Culture and Society

SC

D0928514

0046506446

MOVIE THERAPY

How it changes lives

Bernie Wooder UKCP

© Bernie Wooder 2008
www.themovietherapist.com

Editor: Kathy Lowe
Design: Ed Fredenburgh
Logo design: www.websphere.co.uk
Printed by Lightning Source UK
Published 2008 by Rideau Lakes Publishing

ISBN 978-0-9560751-0-9

For Amber

Acknowledgements

There are four people I especially want to thank for their specific invlovement in the writing of this book: Rachel Pedrithes for her commitment, dependability, for typing faster than I could talk and for giving me honest and valuable feedback; Kathy Lowe, my editor, who is the consumate professional, for keeping me on track and organised; my daughter Claire Johnson for her intelligence, wit and her support with just about everything over the years in the production of this book; and Charles Drazin for his advice, guidance and encouragement.

My thanks go to my wife Joy for her patience, for reading each case study back to me, for listening to me go on about the book and for many cups of tea; to my son Jamie Wooder for his help with the computer and his encouragement; to Pat and Hugh Jones, both retired teachers, who read the draft and gave me valuable feedback; to Peter Malone and Roz Sills who both did earlier editing; and to friends Milton and Elinor Simanowitz and Ann Page for their support and feedback.

About the author

Bernie Wooder was born 6 August 1940 in London's East End. He is a fully trained and UKCP-accredited psychotherapist and counsellor with 20 years' experience and his own private practice. He is qualified in Core Process Psychotherapy, a Buddhist, and until 2004 had a practice in Harley Street.

A film buff from childhood, Bernie Wooder has pioneered the use of movies as an aspect of the therapeutic process for over 15 years. His commissioned work has included consultancy projects on movie therapy for MGM Studios and Warner Brothers and lectures on the subject to student therapists at Guys Teaching Hospital in London and to media students at Leeds Trinity University.

As a member of the UK Council of Psychotherapists he is a regular contributor to TV, radio and press. He has appeared on the BBC's Here and Now and Arena programmes; on Channel 4 and 5 News; on Richard and Judy's Good Morning programme on ITV and on their Channel 4 programme. On radio, promoting the use of movies as a therapeutic tool, he has been interviewed by Professor Anthony Clare on his All in the Mind programme, as well as featuring on Steve Wright in the Afternoon, The Lowri Turner Show and LBC at Midnight.

Bernie lives with his wife Joy, daughter Claire and son Jamie in Boreham Wood, Hertfordshire – appropriately enough on the doorstep of Elstree Film and Television Studios.

CONTENTS

The Healing Power of Movies

Extract from David (Lord) Puttnam's BAFTA Fellowship Acceptance Speech at the Orange British Academy Film Awards, 19 February 2006. Reproduced with his kind permission.

Just a couple of weeks before I won the BAFTA award for *Chariots of Fire* and then went on and won it in Los Angeles, won the Oscar, my Dad had died. And so this charismatic, this extraordinary man and I never had the opportunity to exchange that glance or hug each other. And that left a hole. But movies you know have got an amazing way of detecting those moments. They speak to us. Every single one of you has sat in a movie house and watched some moment of your life healed, or addressed, or touched. Something that you thought that only you knew. There are a number of films I could relate that did this but I've only got time for one.

Bear with me.

I guess a lot of you, I hope a lot of you, saw the movie *The Sixth Sense*. It's a very fine film. Do you remember the final scene when Toni Collette is in the car with her son? She's had a very difficult life, she's a single mother who's had a tough time, and she's had to come to terms with the fact that her son can speak to the spirit world. And the little boy says to her "Mummy, is it true, Grandma told me that shortly after she died you went and visited her graveside?"

And Toni Collette says "Yeah, that's true." "And Grandma said you asked her a question. Is that true?"

She says "Yeah. Yes, I did ask Grandma a question."

"Well," he says, "Grandma wants you to know that the answer to that question is 'Yes, every single day.' But Mum, what was the question?"

Toni Collette starts to cry and through her tears she says "I just asked her if she'd ever been proud of me."

I remember that hitting me like a punch in the stomach. And tonight I know absolutely for sure I never really have to ask the question again but thanks to you and your generosity my Dad's very proud, my family's very proud and I am more proud than I ever believed I could be.

Thank you so much.

The author is grateful to Lord Puttnam for his permission to reproduce this extract from his speech.

INTRODUCTION

We have all seen movies and felt sad or happy after watching them. I have taken this process further, developing the theory that movies can actually help with a range of deep seated problems.

In my experience as a therapist I have found that moments from movies, issues contained within them or relationships between movie characters have helped many of my clients to quickly identify the feelings, and later the reasons, for unconscious unhappiness. So many times a scene has proved a powerful catalyst for unconcious, repressed emotions, and memories. Seeing a mirror image on screen has assisted clients enormously in realising and communicating troubling emotions. Using film as an aid to healing they have gone on to lead much more contented and rewarding lives.

Movie therapy can help with problems such as divorce and relationship difficulties; bereavement; depression and low self esteem; feelings of being unsafe in the world; crisis situations; anxiety, worry and nervousness; shyness and lack of confidence; low motivation; and an inability to relax.

However movie therapy is no quick fix. It is therapy with a trained professional – a specialist equipped to deal with the disturbing feelings that can sometimes be brought to the surface. This was part of my work when I was invited to train therapists at Guys Teaching Hospital in London in aspects of movie therapy. My focus is on the balanced growth of my clients' spiritual and psychological development.

Five detailed case studies and three shorter ones form the

core of this book, presented as my research and evidence for movie therapy. They consist of extracts from, and summaries of, therapy sessions with particular clients who gave permission for their stories to be told. Real names are withheld for confidentiality. In fact, all five clients featured in the longer case studies chose their own 'cover' names.

The case studies reflect how, as part of the clients' therapy, I teach them to develop their awareness to establish mindfulness. Mindfulness is the ability to witness our thoughts, our feelings and our bodily sensations from a detached point of view so we get to observe how they work inside – their process.

What has been especially helpful in assisting clients to be mindful of their process is when I give them 'homework'. I ask them to watch a DVD of a film they have chosen containing scenes which particularly move them. The process I teach them enables them be mindful of their response and to view these scenes repeatedly, gradually reducing the emotional charge from them. Any further emotional expression that may be needed can be worked on in therapy and can include the discovery of further insights.

The case studies of Bette, Mac, Maureen, Tasha and Millie trace these clients' painful journeys back to health over time. Susi, Pennie and Elspeth each helped my research by discussing with me in a single therapy session a chosen film that had made a huge impact on their lives.

All these experiences show the powerful therapeutic role played by movies in the healing process.

Bernie Wooder, October 2008

MAC

Mac's case is a study in terror and its long lasting effect on personality and relationships. Paradoxically this tall, smartly dressed and articulate Scot was still a frightened little boy inside. With Watership Down Mac experienced a life-changing epiphany. He found The Lord of the Rings of great assistance in working with, and understanding, the dynamics of his deep turmoil. Star Wars offered him characters that helped him to manage and express his troubled inner world.

The phone rang one evening. "Is that Bernie Wooder?" the caller asked in a soft Scottish accent.

"Yes it is," I replied.

"My name is Mac and I've been in therapy with Steve. We are ending our sessions as he is moving to Spain. He gave me your telephone number as a therapist he could recommend, so I am wondering, do you have spaces to see me?"

"I'll just get my diary. I have a space at 7pm on Tuesday evenings. Could you make that?"

"Yes that's fine," he said.

I gave him my address and explained that it would be an exploratory session to see if we could work together. He agreed.

As I replaced the receiver I felt his discomfort through the phone. It was quite cleverly concealed but I felt there was something else I couldn't quite put my finger on. Our work had started.

The following evening I came home from my clinic in Golders Green to find an envelope on my mat. It had been delivered by hand by Mac who lives some distance away. To my surprise it contained quite a detailed history of Mac's life and his current preoccupations about coming to see me or continuing with therapy at all.

I found it very interesting that someone would drive 20

miles to deliver something like that the day after a phone call to meet and wondered why. There was a kind of urgency with this situation but at the same time ambivalence on Mac's part about coming at all. I began to realise it was going to be very interesting working with him.

The following day was Mac's appointment. He stood about 6ft tall. His energy was wary, his face somehow held back, chin in, eyes quickly surveying me, a slight smile, hand extended.

"Hello Bernie," he said in his soft Scottish burr.

"Hello Mac. Come in."

In the session room Mac took off his polished brown leather shoes, placing them at an angle to his left, then put his wallet and car keys in the shoe nearest to him. As he went through this methodical routine, he seemed somehow in a world of his own, totally absorbed, as if I wasn't there. This turned out to be the ritual of order that Mac would go through at the beginning of every session.

I began. "This is a getting to know each other session for you to see how you feel with me." I then asked Mac how it felt leaving Steve, his previous therapist.

"Oh you know, sad." He seemed nervous, uncomfortable, just looking at me as if to say 'help me out here'. Bearing in mind the amount of information about himself Mac had sent me, I was trying to gauge a comfortable pace of one-to-one disclosure for him.

"How does it feel meeting me?"

"It feels strange, a bit disorientating really," he said, smiling and looking a bit more comfortable.

"Yes it must do. How long did it take you to end?" I asked, referring to ending therapy with Steve.

"About four weeks."

"Did you feel that was long enough?"

"Yeah, it was OK."

"OK, really? I wonder if you have some other feelings that are not OK?"

Mac waited for a while and sighed. "I think I am sad and angry at the same time. After all, my close relationship with Steve has ended. How can I ever find anyone or anything else to replace that?"

Inside I felt that this was better, more real. It gave me a clearer understanding of what therapy with Steve had meant to Mac. A kind of longing and despair in the question 'how can I find anyone to replace Steve?' seemed to denote this.

After a pause Mac said, "Perhaps that's why there's a lump in my throat at present. It has been around on and off, ever since Tuesday evening which would have normally been the time I spent discussing my issues with Steve." Mac looked directly in my eyes. "Just to make things interesting, I am now seeing you, Bernie, on Tuesday evenings at this time. Yet another yardstick to measure things by."

I was astounded. Somehow I had unknowingly managed to make the same time on the same day for our sessions that Mac had arranged with his previous therapist.

Mac continued, "I'm pissed off because my comfortable routine has been disrupted. Also I am feeling the terrible onset of deep seated anxiety."

"What are you anxious about?"

Mac paused. "If I'm going to make a go of this, if I'm going to be open with you about what I am feeling. It raises many questions in me."

"What kind of questions?"

"Well, why do I want to see a therapist? This question has got me vexed for the moment. I've scrambled around for reasons, ideas, thoughts – possibly trying to justify my actions to myself. Seems to be a common theme in my life, this self-doubt."

His face clouded over with anxiety. "Self-doubt, anxiety and apprehension are not uncommon feelings and I'm not alone in experiencing them but something does not feel healthy." He moved around restlessly and sighed.

"Mac, I'm feeling a little confused. What is the something that does not feel healthy?"

Mac replied somewhat testily, "The circumstances of my childhood; the atmosphere; the lack of guidance and support. All served as bloody good reasons not to trust or show any part of my emotional self to anyone."

"How does that make you feel?"

"Cut off from people and from myself," he said despairingly. Then he got quite angry. "Here I am contemplating revealing myself to someone I know next to nothing about. Fuck. Even if you, Bernie, do know Steve and Steve knows you, what does that mean? That I'll feel we can work together? Or even that you can work with me? I am busy torturing myself with this idea."

"I'm a bit confused Mac. Which idea?"

Mac completely disregarded my question and continued,

"Already I'm trying to gauge you, yet I have absolutely nothing to go on. Dick all. Zilch. Zero. In my mind I'm wondering how you will measure up against my experience with Steve. After all I did spend two years and seven months seeing him on a once a week basis. I know I covered a lot of ground with him, not plain sailing but beneficial nevertheless." He was moving from side to side in the armchair fists clenched unconciously and stuttering slightly at times.

I glanced at the clock. We were just about two minutes until the end, not enough time to address any of the questions lining up in my mind.

"Well, we'll just have to take it gradually to see if you feel you can work with me and to see if I feel I can work with you. But I must say, Mac, I have no reservations on my side. We have about two minutes to go before we end and I don't want to raise anymore questions at present."

Mac looked up, smiled, looked relieved and started to put his shoes on.

Mac's history

Mac arrived and again, as I opened the door, his face subtly moved back as if he were waiting for a problem. I noted this subtle facial and bodily movement. "Come in Mac."

Mac sat down, surveying the room as he leaned back in the chair. This survey of the room was total. He took in every object, ensuring that the door was closed. He checked the windows and even checked me out, looking deeply into my eyes and remaining silent for a while. I felt like I was in the presence of someone who had been in the Special Air Service (SAS).

I asked myself what this man was trying to establish. Then after a moment the answer just popped into my head. It seemed so obvious – it was safety – he was checking his surroundings in every session to ensure that he was safe. This explained why he was the only client to bring his shoes into the session room. He needed to have his shoes with him in case he had to run.

"Can you tell me about your childhood Mac?" Mac's right hand became a fist.

"My childhood was miserable," he said in a grey voice. "I'm becoming more and more aware of its full horror. Memories come back to me of my father beating my mother up. There was a regular cycle of mother leaving, taking myself and my sister to stay with a maternal Gran when things went too far. She always ended up going back, saying things would be different this time. I lost count of the number of times this pattern repeated itself. Five times possibly. I don't know and tried not to care."

This was a disturbing story already. The tone of Mac's voice, the involuntary jumps of his body as he talked and the fact that it was a dark winter night outside, with the trees throwing shadows on my garden, only added to the cold, hatred-filled atmosphere developing in the room.

"My father was violent, threatening, terrifying – an unpredictable bully with a short fuse. He only ever targeted my mother with his physical and verbal abuse and made sure he destroyed and damaged her possessions when in one of his deranged moods."

Mac went very quiet. I just sat there, letting him have his space to think and remember but not feel pressured in any way.

Mac continued, "It has taken me a long time to realise his behaviour was not normal and that he was mentally unbalanced during these times." Then, as an afterthought, he said, "Not that I could relate to his behaviour prior to or post these periods. I think he used alcohol to deaden his inner pain, a pain that was often unleashed upon my family with disastrous consequences for my mum."

Mac's knuckles went white as he clenched his fists unconsciously. The atmosphere in the room became even more tense while all this poured out of him.

He looked incredibly angry now and his voice rose. "Fuck. How I hated and despised him. My father was a monster whom I somehow felt totally ashamed of and responsible for – one who scared the living daylights out of me. It was like living on the slopes of a volcano about to erupt. I was, and I still am, fearful of the memory I hold of him."

Mac went quiet, his breathing very laboured. "My father joined the army when he was young. He was in the Royal Scots Parades as a piper for 10 years plus. From what I know he carried on with other women even when he was going out with my mum and was violent towards her from the start. Why do I think that?" he questioned himself. "Why did my mum stay with him?" The questions kept coming. "What did she see in him? I feel angry and resentful towards her for this."

As I sat there listening, the chaotic childhood that Mac was describing reverberated through me emotionally and mentally. I noticed my own hands were clenched into fists.

Then Mac, his face softer now, said surprisingly, "I would like to know more about his life in the army as a piper – to feel proud of him – but all that is too late now. All I can remember in my childhood was the actual violence or the impending threat of it."

"Mac, how did you cope with all this?"

He looked at me and sighed. He had coped, he explained, by withdrawing, in the belief that all violence, contentious issues and strong emotions were to be avoided. He thought he was unaffected by it all, never sharing with anyone his thoughts and feelings on family life. Until now, that is. "I did well at school academically and I was always the quiet one good at sports and athletics. That was a saving grace I feel."

"Yes, I think it probably was." I was thinking how helpful physical exercise and exertion can be in dealing with depression, frustration and repressed violence in a non-harmful way. If Mac had not followed this path, he would be acting in the same way as his dad.

Mac went on to tell me he found relationships difficult and felt wary around everyone. "It is like I don't know or understand the rules of the game." As he said this he looked tremendously troubled and was gripping his hand into a fist. He continued to move around restlessly.

Inside, I sensed the complete isolation that Mac must experience every moment of his life. He must feel permanently on edge, wrong footed, out of step.

Mac continued, "Father and mother are now divorced and all contact with the past is gone, thank Christ. Mother is now outgoing. She's always been a good listener and genuine with her emotions and sharing them. I've noticed the little differences each time I go home. She's been in a stable relationship for 10 years and I marvel at the way she and her partner argue and disagree with one another while still maintaining a healthy, balanced relationship."

Then, as an afterthought, Mac said with a smile, "Can you still have boyfriends at 60? They have houses on each side of Glasgow, both with no intentions of moving. I feel very wary around her partner; the unconscious memory of my father afflicts me. According to my mum I am distant and very difficult to reach – I can relate to that."

"Ever since I've moved down south, mum has always maintained regular contact. She is constant, she supports me in whatever I decide to do, even when I deliberately ignore her and am angry towards her. She does not cry and she will answer my questions regarding her relationship with my father. She flies down from Scotland to visit me three or four times a year. I'm glad she invites herself because I don't know if I could ask her to visit as I'm not that confident about asking her for things I want."

"What is difficult about asking?"

Mac had a pained expression on his face now as if he could not talk. His mouth was open, trying to get the words out, and he started to stammer. This articulate man suddenly became like a hesitant child. And once again this important new development showed itself just as we were reaching the end of the session.

I suggested that we talk more about this next time. He glanced at me, a look of relief gradually coming into his eyes. He took a deep sigh, leaned forward and reached for his shoes. "OK," he said, quietly lost in a world of his own.

A child's needs neglected

As Mac sat there today, eyeing me with cold hateful eyes, my mind wandered back to the previous session where he had talked about his mum.

"Mac, you were talking about your mum in the last session and I would like you to tell me more about her, about your relationship with her."

Mac turned red. He looked restless and agitated and was muttering under his breath, "Fuck me; fuck me Bernie; this is difficult."

"What's difficult?"

Pain and frustration clouded his face as he tried desperately to communicate. He suddenly blurted out, "We didn't have a fucking relationship, that was just it."

After a long silence I asked, "What was 'just it' Mac? What do you mean?"

Mac's face started to twitch involuntarily. I felt that whatever he was going through must be huge. Finally he said, "The problem was she could never, ever, be there for me. But…" he started to breathe more heavily, move about more restlessly "… what made it worse, what made it so fucking worse, was at moments when I really needed her to comfort me, to reassure me, she wasn't there. She wanted *me* to comfort her." He spoke in a high pitched, exasperated voice.

"That must have been terrible, Mac. How did it make you feel?"

He thought for a moment and then started to stutter pitifully. "Like I was falling... round and round... into an abyss. Like in one of those dreams." As I looked at this huge man I saw him diminish into a terrorised little boy. It was very sad to see this level of suffering.

Mac looked totally drained so I suggested we rest for a while.

I had been somewhat surprised at the power and onslaught of the experience he related and could see no point in re-traumatising him further at that moment. Gradually Mac's colour started to normalise as he began to talk more easily again and there was a sense of relief about him. I just carried on the rest of the session with comforting small talk to help him to prepare for the outside world and the drive home.

As he left and as I started to reflect on the experiences he had shared with me I realised that this was only one aspect of Mac's suffering. I wondered how he'd come through it so articulate and intact in many ways. He must be very strong because he had also been forced to deal with his father's hair-trigger violence. What must it have been like to grow up with all of that? At those moments of the dad's violence or Mac's need, his mother's emotional level was that of a traumatised little girl, so she went with her needs to Mac, blind to his need for comfort and reassurance. It made me wonder whether there had been violence and abuse in his mother's own upbringing.

I then started to list what I thought were the beliefs that governed Mac's life. They were:

1. No one's there for me
2. Trust no one
3. Depend only on yourself
4. Always be on guard
5. Never, ever, drop your guard and be vulnerable – that's when you get hurt.

He later admitted that he felt like he was in no man's land in the First World War, crawling between enemy lines with no protection and no defence between the trenches – facing certain death at any moment.

On the march

On this particular evening Mac sat shoulders slumped, very heavily depressed and not talking at all. This, in turn, made me feel restless.

After some time I decided to share my feelings of restlessness. Mac just looked at me contemptuously as if to say 'that's your problem'.

"I wonder if you feel like that inside, Mac?"

"Nope, I don't," he said, still fixing me with a stare.

About 10 minutes from the end of the session I made a clinical decision. "Mac, I am still feeling restless. Can you notice the heaviness in the room?"

Before I could finish he said disdainfully, "Yes, I noticed you're jumping about all over the place." There was a look of sadistic pleasure at my discomfort and a thin smile played across his face. The atmosphere in the room was becoming increasingly oppressive – so much so that it was somehow difficult to breathe. Mac was sitting still and very sullen. The unbearable heaviness was Mac's, I knew, and I decided I had contained it long enough.

So I got up and marched up and down the room saying, "Well, someone has to unblock it."

Mac was absolutely astonished. His eyes were wide open, body energy now alive, no more slumping. A smile came to his face. I carried on dutifully marching up and down the room in at a pace that was needed to release the restlessness and heaviness I was feeling.

"This is not in the manual!" Mac roared, tears of laughter streaming down his face as I continued marching up and down. Then he collapsed laughing.

I sat down. "That's done it I think." Now in front of me I had a new Mac, full of fun and warmth-connected.

All heaviness gone, he was energised and relaxed. He got up, still laughing, a look of wonderment and amazement on his face and as he said goodbye he waved in the friendliest manner he had ever shown towards me.

Liberation and spiritual awakening

During a following session Mac began telling me about a particular time at home.

"One evening, Bernie, the atmosphere was tense. My dad found a reason to pick on my mum. He shouted abuse at her, building himself up into a fury, then raised his hands to punch and slap her.

"I'd watched this scene in paralysed terror many times, but this time I felt different, I felt the terror. There was now something deeper, stronger in me fuelled by protective hatred and revenge. I faced my dad and said, 'NO MORE!' He looked astonished but I could feel every cell of my being vibrating with hatred and rage towards him. I was 15 years old and wanted this to end now. My father stopped, looked at me for a moment and walked away. My mum looked too – nothing like this had ever happened before."

"Mac, you transcended any feelings of terror. You stood directly in front of your mum and gave your dad a look that said, 'NO, it ends here, now, today, your reign of terror is over'."

"Yes, that's it. Then I just stood there, calm, solid and centred."

The balance of power in the house had changed forever. Mac's courageous act was a spiritual awakening for him for he had connected with a power greater than his fears. He broke out into beads of sweat as he contemplated the dangerous thing he had done.

I was transfixed. It was a very dramatic session and the temperature in the room had shot up. I sat there humbled by Mac's trauma – by the exceptional way he had transcended his suffering to find a depth of spirituality in the face of terror.

We were now at the end of the session. Mac looked quite shaky as he was leaving. "Bye Mac," I said. "Bye," he replied, apparently miles away as he walked off.

When he had gone I reflected on a passage from Joseph Campbell's Myths To Live By in which he quotes the German philosopher Arthur Schopenhauer:

"How is it, he [Schopenhauer] asks, that an individual can so forget himself and his own safety that he will put himself and his life in jeopardy to save another from death or pain – as though that other's life were his own, that other's danger his own? Such a one is then acting, Schopenhauer answers, out of an instinctive recognition of the truth that he and that other in fact are one. He had been moved not from the lesser, secondary knowledge of himself as separate from others, but from an immediate experience of the greater, truer truth, that we are all one in the ground of our being. Schopenhauer's name for this motivation is "compassion," mitleid, and he identifies it as the one and only inspiration of inherently moral action. It is founded, in his view, in a metaphysically valid insight. For a moment one is selfless, boundless, without ego. And I have lately had occasion to think frequently of this word of Schopenhauer as I have watched on television newscasts those heroic helicopter rescues, under fire in Vietnam, of young men wounded in enemy territory: their fellows, forgetful of their own safety, putting their young lives in peril as though the lives to be rescued were their own. There, I would say – if we are looking truly for an example in our day – is an authentic rendition of the labour of love."[1]

This, I think, was precisely Mac's experience.

Watership Down and Bigwig's sacrifice

At the tail-end of a recent session I had asked Mac if any film had moved him by touching on his experiences. He had replied matter-of-factly, though he had never mentioned it before, "Oh yes, *Watership Down*." So, I decided that I would continue this dialogue with him about the film.

When Mac arrived, he looked around the room, eyed me suspiciously and took in every detail. I was thinking he would have made a wonderful SAS soldier. "Well," he said, and sighed. He sat quietly, right hand seeming to jump and twitch until it turned into a customary fist.

"Mac, if you haven't got anything immediate, could we talk about your experience of watching *Watership Down?*"

He looked quite pleased. "Oh, yeah." He took a deep breath, sat back to get comfortable and released his fist. "Well, Bernie, it all feels so simple, so straightforward. A depiction of events in an animated cartoon involving rabbits struggling against injustice." Mac's face clouded over and the mood of the room changed.

"My memories, my unrecognised feelings, were brought into conscious awareness from watching *Watership Down*." I felt fascinated that this big man who'd known almost the limits of human suffering had found help in a cartoon. For me this was a first. Mac went on, "I read the book when I was in my teens and even then it moved me greatly. It brought up such profound feelings about the battle for justice and freedom in the face of tyranny and terror."

Mac explained that the book *Watership Down* by Richard Adams, upon which the film is based, concerns a group of rabbits leaving their hitherto cosy but ultimately doomed warren and setting out in search of a new warren where they could live safely. He continued, "It's a story of self discovery, a venture of loyalty, trust, and for me the willingness to make a sacrifice in defence of individual rights."

Mac paused for a while: his face went a bit pale. He stared at the floor and continued, "What can I say, what can I do other than tell you my feelings surrounding the scene in which the two rabbits, Bigwig and General Wound-Wort fight for control? It may seem simple but the underlying theme is of great importance for me."

Mac swallowed. "Bigwig is one of those who leaves the established warren in search of a new place to live. Even though he is stronger, possesses knowledge of the world at large and has leadership experience, it's not him who leads the band but another rabbit called Hazel. Hazel possesses a quality that Bigwig is yet to realise. It's one of care and compassion for those around him no matter who they are. Bigwig reluctantly agrees to follow Hazel, but plans to usurp his leadership at the first opportunity."

I was truly fascinated at the unfolding of this story and Mac's complete comprehension of it. Mac continued, "The rabbits come face to face with an oppressive force in the shape of General Wound-Wort, intent on subjugating them and eradicating all independent rights." I noticed both Mac's hands had turned into fists, knuckles white. He was now breathing much faster. "General Wound-Wort runs his warren in military precision, maintained through a regime of harshness and terror." Mac's hate looked palpable now. "His word is law, above questioning and discussion. In short, he is a dictator."

I looked at the clock. Good, we still had quite a lot of time. Mac went on, "By the time of the confrontation, Bigwig has put to one side his leadership aspirations and is united with the other group members in defending themselves against the General and his vastly superior army of followers. The General is fierce, intent on destroying all those who oppose him. It is this scene which moves me greatly." Mac paused and I was on tenterhooks.

Mac said very firmly, "Bigwig faces up to the General, defending and protecting the group less able than he is. Although he is the biggest in the group, Bigwig is still smaller and no match for the General. Both rabbits know this, yet Bigwig stands by his decision to defend the group. In a crucial moment Bigwig acknowledges this and his loyalty to the group leader Hazel. For me it's symbolic of the battle for the right to be heard and to openly possess individual thoughts without intimidation or retribution. It is also about standing up for what is morally right."

I was transfixed by Mac's identification with the terror and oppressive ways of the General. Clearly this paralleled his feelings about his violent father.

Mac's voice broke. "The scene moves on and the tears are flowing down my cheeks. I recognise the significance of what I am watching and find it climactic and disturbing." Mac's face now looked flushed. "Bigwig's struggle, my struggle, all intertwined. A battle is raging in my heart, yet I understand Bigwig's motivation. It's in defence of others physically less able than himself and lies above and beyond any idea of personal gain or safety."

My mind immediately flashed back to Mac's confrontation with his father.

Mac's voice cracked now. "Such a sacrifice," he said, "such grief, such suffering. No person can ask that of another – it can only be undertaken voluntarily. Righteousness shall prevail but it takes courage to make it happen."

The hairs stood up on my arms. I was intensely moved at the emotional identification Mac had made with Bigwig facing the General, and himself at the age of 15 facing his dad to protect his mother. The clarity of that experience of sacrifice was being lived out in front of me. Mac went on, "In the blink of an eye, the understanding of what I had seen crystallised my memories and feelings. I felt deeply moved as I gained a new perspective on a major event in my life, a perspective that recognises and assigns."

Mac paused, looking out the window. I realised time was moving on. He continued, "The scene drew importance to my actions in a time of great terror. Understanding comes in many forms... it takes a willingness and desire to look deep within oneself to realise this. In the story Bigwig survives the battle with the General."

I looked up at the clock and noticed we were right on time. Mac looked emotionally drained. I felt how important this film had been to Mac's healing and liberation from his terrible suffering. As we got to the door Mac stopped, looked at me for the first time and said in a small voice, "Can I have a hug?"

"Sure," I said, and I noticed as I hugged him that his body was riddled with tension.

"Bye, Bernie, see you next week."

I closed the door feeling stunned at the enormity of what I had just heard.

Mac faces death

It was a dark, blustery evening when Mac arrived. He looked apprehensive as he walked in, his large frame and tall straight walk filling my hallway.

His eyes checked every aspect of the room. He was in deep thought as he did his customary ritual – shoes to the left with car keys inside them.

After Mac had agreed for his case study to go into this book, I used to write up his story at regular intervals and give it to him for his observations on accuracy and for his agreement. As a spin off, this gave the therapy greater depth.

Mac started by saying, "What you wrote about me and our session a few weeks ago helped me so much. It enabled me to cry, which I find extremely difficult."

"Do you have a support group?" I asked.

"Yes, that's where I took it. I read it out to a few of them." A wave of compassion went through me. He was referring to the case study for this book that I had given him for his approval. In it I had written about his supreme act of courage and sacrifice in facing up to his father to protect his mother.

"Bernie," Mac cried despairingly, "what's happening to me, I feel so confused?" He paused. "I am in chaos." He now had his head in his hands.

"I am here Mac. It's the shock coming out after all these years." Gently I asked, "Do you have any association that comes up around this chaos, any memory?"

Mac looked ashen. "I faced death and my mum and dad…" he paused, sighed, looking from side to side in utter exasperation…"they carried on around me…like I was not there. Fuck. What does she want from me?"

He got up now, pacing up and down and stuttering pitifully.

The energy that filled the room was titanic, oppressive. I breathed, relaxed, stayed in the moment to get a sense of peace in myself. To witness such suffering was an incredibly humbling experience.

Mac's colour started to return to his face. He looked calmer now.

"How do you feel?"

"I feel," Mac answered quietly "like the level of threat I was just experiencing has dropped."

"Much?"

"From about 100 per cent to 50 per cent."

"Yes, OK." Inside I still felt his radar scanning energy for danger, still active.

We both suddenly started coughing. The room was now sweltering and I was desperate to go to the toilet. I shared this with Mac who laughed in disbelief and relief at my disclosure. Ending time was near so I opened the patio doors to let in the crisp night air.

Mac's life as opera

Mac arrived for his session looking as dark as thunder, glowering around the room. He looked at me with a sneer and then said, "I want to pick on something. I want to pick on you. Everything is wrong."

He went on in his strong Scottish accent, "I just can't get rid of it. I just can't get rid of it." He was moving his hands, flicking them, as though something was stuck to them. As he flicked his hands, he bared his teeth. He unconsciously brought up his right hand in a claw and growled.

I had the distinct feeling of 'unbearableness'. This unbearable feeling was my sense of what was stuck to Mac. He can't get away from it whatever he does.

Mac looked at me contemptuously then looked away. He had started to remember things that had helped him from previous sessions. If he got up and paced, this would allow him to use up more of his energy. He said, "I am fucking getting up, I can't stand sitting here." He started to pace up and down, to claw and growl. I asked him to exaggerate the clawing and the growling because it seemed the best expression of the animalistic rage he felt. So, by expressing this, it could afford him at least some relief.

He said, "I am just so full of energy." I asked where this energy was. "In my legs." I had an idea but as soon as I had it I also knew that Mac would not agree to it.

"Mac, there is something you can try if you like to, that might help."

"Yeah," he said sullenly, "what is it?"

"Well, if you lie on the floor and just let your legs express that energy in a running motion..."

Mac cut me off as I was speaking and regarded me with incredulity. As he looked at me with this questioning expression I felt a smile creeping up inside me.

"That's fucking mad. Do you think I'm going to lie down and fucking do that? How's that going to help me, pretending to fucking run?" Inside me the smile was growing bigger.

"Well, it's difficult to tell you the experience before you have it and to have it you have to do it."

I had found this technique helpful when working with women who had been raped. The trapped feeling in the legs is adrenaline, the fight or flight response. In the sense of running or by closing your eyes, you start to release that energy. This can often afford you some emotional relief and may trigger memories that are helpful.

"But you don't have to do it, it's your choice."

Mac sat down on the floor grudgingly. In a little boy's voice, he whined and rocked back and forth as he sat. "I'm not going to fucking do it. No, I'm not fucking doing it."

All of it was said like a child sulking and having a tantrum. Suddenly, he got up, and started marching up and down. Then he leant on the back of an arm chair, face now blood red, twisting his body into all sorts of awkward shapes and contortions. It was clear that there was some huge struggle going on inside him. Mac doesn't always tell me what he's struggling with inside, but he lets me facilitate him dealing with it. "Boy," he said suddenly, "it's so hot in here. I am sweating, my hands are sweating." Mac's colour can change dramatically within a given session and he now had a grey-like pallor that made him look quite unwell.

After seeing that struggle for so long I said, "Mac, it's been our experience in other sessions that physical contact helps you."

Mac looked at me and said, "I'm not coming over there." I moved forward about an inch to adjust my back. Mac, who was right across the room, glared at me with the clear message that I should stay where I was. "I wondered what you were going to do then."

"Yes I did slightly move, but I was adjusting my posture because I currently have a bad back."

Mac listened like he couldn't care less about my back. He stood there for a while, swaying backwards and forwards. Then he said, "I want to come over there but I can't. My legs won't move. I am rooted to the spot."

"OK, just stay there and if you don't come it doesn't matter."

Suddenly, Mac just walked over slowly and sat down like a little boy on the side of my armchair. I placed my hand gently on his left shoulder and asked, "Is that OK?" (It is so important to check with physical touch and not assume you are doing the right thing. The client will tell you.)

Mac whispered that it was, then a frightening thing happened. His whole face started to twitch involuntarily. He started to blink incredibly fast. I was greatly moved at seeing his suffering. I was so aware of all this turmoil in Mac's mind that I decided simply to stroke his hair in a gentle way, as you would a child. But I asked Mac first if that would be

OK. He said 'yes' quietly. I hardly touched his hair but just enough to feel the contact of the stroke. Time was getting on now but Mac started to calm down, his twitching stopped slowly.

Mac decided to get up and sit down in his usual chair opposite me. When he looked at me almost pleadingly and reached out like he had done before, I gently took his hand and looked into his eyes. He looked back to mine, searching. He had to see my care and it was important that he saw the sincerity in my eyes.

He saw the truth of what I felt for him and his suffering and seemed a little calmer, though still full of angst and despair. I had a momentary thought that the time was getting on now and that we had to end. Because the room was sweltering on this summer evening, I imagined going out into my garden with Mac, letting him feel the cool night air as I know he likes the fountain with the Buddha presiding over it.

Mac immediately noticed and asked, "What happened there – how are you feeling? You looked uncomfortable. Are you bored?"

"No Mac," I responded clearly and firmly, "I am not bored. I was realising that we were about to run over time and we had to end the session, but at the same time I had the vision of the two of us walking out to the garden, to the fountain, to the Buddha I have in my garden."

What followed next was quite incredible. Mac smiled slowly with a look of total disbelief and pleasure mixed. He said, "That's fucking great." He then started to laugh, doubled up with real belly laughs. "Thank you. It's not what you said: it's that you told me what you were thinking."

With that I said, "OK, let's be naughty," and we walked out together into the cool evening breeze, which was in such a marked contrast to the sweltering room. We were there only a few minutes until Mac turned round to leave and we walked back together. He was laughing all the way, different energy, a different person altogether now.

As he got to the door, ready to go, this huge man of 6'2" looked down at my 5'2" and asked, "Can we have a hug?"

We hugged and I felt Mac's body tremble as though he had relaxed just that little bit more. "Bye Bernie," he said lightly, "see you next week," and carried on laughing as if he could not believe it.

Wormtongue and Gandalf

It was about 6.50pm. Waiting for Mac to arrive I recalled how, in the previous session, we had worked very much with his fear of silence, his whole approach to silence, how anxious it made him. We looked at it step by step and though Mac had found this very difficult and had tried to resist, in the end he said he felt as clean as a piece of pine. When I asked him whether that was good, bad or neutral, he said, "Oh, good." This is placid Mac. To get information from him about something like this is like pulling teeth. Nonetheless he clearly felt something important had happened in the session.

Unusually, in the last few weeks, Mac has sent me a couple of letters and a couple of emails. I was excited because he told me he had found The Lord of the Rings becoming more and more helpful to him. Previously Mac had only ever talked about Watership Down, so this introduction of a new film was very interesting.

When Mac arrived I noticed him move his face back just a couple of inches in his instinctive wariness. He carried out his ritual of looking round every inch of the room, checking everything, taking his shoes off and putting his car keys and wallet in his left shoe. He then gave me a look, somewhat searching and somewhat aggressive. "What are those?" he asked, pointing to some throat pastels that I had on my right hand side, "dog biscuits or something?" The tone had a subtle edge of sarcasm and the lips very subtly curled as he spoke. If there is such a thing a semi snarl, this was it!

I simply replied, "They are for my throat as it gets a bit irritated sometimes."

Mac said, "Oh," in a tone so markedly agreeable that there was quite a contrast between this and the tone of his opening words.

"Bernie, after our last session, something occurred to me – a way of seeing things." Mac was referring to imagery from The Lord of the Rings which he had mentioned to me briefly in previous sessions. "Wormtongue is the advisor to the King of Rohan, but his influence is much more powerful than that of advisor. He has the king under his control. As a result the king is wizened, feeble, weak and his eyesight is clouded over by cataracts. He speaks Wormtongue's words, and is unable to function independently. Wormtongue is an unhealthy influence, a poisoner and corrupter of minds."

I recalled that Grima Wormtongue's words constantly whispered in the king's ear had the effect of draining the king of any energy and autonomy. He became Wormtongue's puppet and remained in a kind of depressed stupor most of the time.

I thought how very interesting it was that this man in front of me, who could be reduced to pitiful stuttering, was so articulate and logical in communicating the intricacies and mood of this film.

Then Mac spoke of Gandalf the White, the Wizard for Good, who had the power to dispel Wormtongue's effect on the king. "Gandalf releases the king's mind from the grip of Wormtongue's words, whereupon the king wakes up from his hypnotised state of mind, his eyesight clears and he regains control of himself and his physical strength. Now, free from the distorting influence of Wormtongue, the king wishes to hear Gandalf's opinion much to the bitter resentment of his advisor. Wormtongue, seen for the sly manipulator he is, finds himself cast out."

My question to Mac was, "Who is Wormtongue, who is Gandalf?"

He stood up. "I'm feeling restless."

"Good, just feel your energy and follow through." This was the pattern we used when Mac was becoming angry or restless. He looked across the room and made direct eye contact.

"Are you Gandalf?" he asked in a searching, testing way,

as if I had suggested that I was.

I noticed a look on Mac's face of one who has set a trap for you and is pretty sure you are going to walk into it. "What do you think?" I paused for a moment and then slowly added, "That's what your mind has come up with."

He smiled slowly. "Touché." This answer indicated to me that I had not walked into his trap.

If I had agreed that I was Gandalf, I felt that Wormtongue and Gandalf would not have remained together as the negative and positive parts of Mac's psyche. He would not then have sensed his own power to put things right by tackling his inner Wormtongue.

Later, on the phone, referring to this session, Mac said he had found it 'very deep – maybe too deep'. He wondered whether he should stop coming to see me.

"We can talk about that in the next session." I told him, as I had done at regular intervals, that I was concerned he was doing too much therapy. Independent of me, he was going to workshops and also seeing a craniosacral therapist. The personal impact on him of The Lord of the Rings as well as all this therapy made me fear he was overwhelming himself by bringing up too much powerful material.

I felt he should reduce his workshops so that when he left therapy he would know that he could function properly. I also talked about cutting down on the craniosacral therapy which, though quite gentle, can bring up a great deal. I suggested that he go to see his GP to get some prescriptive medicine to help him with the high level of anxiety he was feeling.

I also advised that he didn't have to be so stoic in facing all this horrible emotion.

Quick as a flash Mac came back at me. "Stoic. I will have to look that up in my dictionary, Bernie," he said, somewhat annoyed.

"OK," I replied, "it means someone who is hard on themselves, who endures rather than seeks help. Be more compassionate to yourself. There is no reason why you can't go to the doctor and get some medication to temporarily help you through this period as you did before. You don't have to do it all on your own and you do need to be around more people who are not in therapy."

Now Mac seemed to want to get off the phone. "Bye," I said, "see you next week."

At our next session Mac told me something had happened to him a while after our phone call. "It suddenly all passed, I felt totally better."

"You came out of your depression and the horrible feelings?" I asked. "Yes," he said. "Not long after that the realisation of *The Lord of the Rings* and Gandalf came to me."

"So, it sounds like you've found your inner Gandalf who has answered the trance of your inner Wormtongue. Is that what's happened do you think?"

Mac looked at me, turned his head sideward, eyed me suspiciously and said, "You are being very slippery, Bernie."

"How?"

"Well, the things you are saying to me."

"Yes, I'm just saying things to you to see if they click or not. Only you know your inner truth and I am trying to help you to find it."

I was noting Mac's incredible awareness and his fear that I was trying to manipulate him – except that those words didn't form quickly enough for me to say that to him in the session.

Mac came and sat down, fixing me again with a stare. "One of the scenes that keeps coming back to me, in *The Lord of the Rings*, is the mailed fist of the warrior who throws the ring into the air and catches it as he considers throwing it into the volcano." I noticed Mac doing the fist and catching the ring with his right hand unconsciously.

"Mac," I said, "can you keep doing that with your fist, opening and closing as you catch the ring, but really become it, really exaggerate it?" Mac did. "Stay with the feeling it gives you."

Mac looked very powerful now and said, "Fuck it, that's what it makes me feel. I know what I believe." A look of wonder passed across his face as I asked him to say that again. He did. "Fuck it!" he said more strongly, shoulders straightening up, jaw jutting out. He went very quiet and the look of wonder stayed on his face.

After a while he said, kind of to himself, "That's it...I realised sitting here that just before I felt better I let go of my depression. That was when I kept seeing that image."

"And those words?" I asked.

"Fuck it, I know what I believe."

"Is it your strength? Is that what helped you?"

"Yes," he said, "in retrospect it did."

"Mac," I inquired, "was it after this experience of your

depression going that you had the insight about Wormtongue and Gandalf and, if so, how long after?"

Mac's eyes were now wide like a little boy's. "Not long after, and I just had to email you and share it with you."

"But I am left still wondering if you found your inner Gandalf that gave you the strength to step out of your depression or your Wormtongue trance. Just something for you to think on or reject Mac."

Mac eyed me suspiciously, and then looked softly at me, showing a great deal of affection. He then said, "Bernie, you are the X factor in this, in my healing."

"Oh," I said, "do you know how I am?"

"Not yet," he said.

"Oh well, there is no rush."

Mac's face flitted to anger and kindness in a split second as he said to me, "I didn't know whether to give you a slap or kiss you when you said that." Inside I was a little surprised, but felt very comfortable.

"Do you feel like that in a lot of your relationships? That is, you often feel you don't know whether to slap or kiss anyone?" Mac's face clouded over. He sighed, and with a sense of relief said, "All the time Bernie, all the time." There was such weariness now and sadness in his tone. I felt very moved for him.

"All I feel is dissatisfaction. How long? How long?" he cried out. "I've been doing all this stuff for five years – maybe longer. Two and a half years with Steve, my previous therapist, four years of weekend primary integration workshops, nearly two years with you, and I still feel dissatisfied."

"Mac, can you tell me what you feel behind that statement you've just made? What are the feelings? What are the words, if you can find any?"

He looked at me with resignation." It's inevitable."

"Is there more to that?"

"Yes," he said, "it will always be there. It's inevitable."

"There," I said quite firmly, "is the negative belief that brings all that feeling about. That is Wormtongue in you speaking. If you believe it won't change, it won't. If you believe it will change, it will. We have to focus on that negative belief that causes you so much suffering."

Inside I was experiencing some very uncomfortable feelings I couldn't define. Then Mac said, "You are the X factor in this. You always give me something, always meet me at whatever depth I am in myself. You are not fazed with anything I throw at you."

As if on queue, I look at the clock and we are just about to go over time. Mac knows this too but will push me a little longer if I let him. "Oh well, thank you Mac. We are coming to the end now." Mac got ready slowly and said goodbye.

I was left with a kind of sick numbness in my chest. I shuddered. So this is what it feels like to be Mac.

Mac confronts his sub-personalities

Mac arrived today looking restless and angry. Before he sat down he couldn't wait to say to me, "I want to find something wrong – to find things wrong here. I want to argue with you."

As he sat down, he hit the Buddha that I'd lent him on the head with his hand, many times over, seemingly unaware of doing it. He had told me in previous sessions that he takes the Buddha to his weekend workshops on primal integration and calls it Bernie. It represents me.

I think I am going to tell him what I am seeing him do. I said, "Mac, do you realise that you are hitting the Buddha that you tell me represents me? How angry you are with me – but you don't show it here. You split off at these weekend workshops and once again I am encouraging you not to do that but to show me now." Mac stared back at me in vibrant, sneering contempt. Inside I was thinking, 'yes, he's angry with me alright'.

Realising this huge man had all this anger running through him, I suggested that he get up and pace, using up this energy.

"Why?" he sneered back at me. "Are you bothered or something? What's behind your suggestion?" He was staring hatefully at me.

"You seem to be overwhelmed with this anger and pacing has helped you in past sessions." Mac looked at me and started pacing – up and down.

Then he said, "I want to kill, I want to destroy, I want to crush. I don't want any fucking sensitivity. Pooffy or nice, I want mechanical things that are heavy or strong. I want thick strong buildings that withstand anything."

He reminds me of the Nazis and worshipping the will. The room was stifling as he marched up and down, clawing at the air and growling and spitting out venomous, poisonous profanities. He was caught up in animalistic revulsion – the beast in him as he called it.

He looked up and said, "I feel like I'm possessed." My reaction was to see this hate as a burning acid fuelling the primeval savagery.

Then suddenly, after expressing all of this, hands shaking, face white, he looked at me like a frightened little boy with a kind of pleading in his eyes. He lowered his head a bit and asked, "Can I sit down next to you?"

Mac sat down like a child to the left side of my armchair. He wanted my hand on his shoulder, contact for reassurance to ground him. After a while he said, "I feel like I need some body work. If I lie down this energy will be OK."

"Alright," I said, and he lay down, face flinching. After a while he added, "I feel it will help if you put your finger in the middle of my forehead."

"Third eye?" I asked.

He just smiled. I gently circled his mid-forehead with my finger. For a while his whole body shook and twitched, then he calmed down and his breathing normalised.

Looking calmer, he decided to sit up.

"I split them off."

"Who?"

"My own personal Jekyll and Hyde."

This was Mac's reference to one side of him being a small boy and one side being his dad. His sub-personalities. He looked very serene as he got up, took his keys out of his shoes, put his wallet in his pocket and left.

Following this session I received an email from Mac:

"Bernie,

"I had a mindful of images last night, all revolving around hunger and emotional need. The first one is right at the forefront of my conscious mind — it's the scene from The Lord of the Rings when the story of the ring's near-destruction is being retold. Men and Elves have united to fight Sauron and his demon allies. They have managed to chop the ring from his hand in the midst of battle.

"It falls upon the King of Men to hurl the ring into the volcano, the only thing which can destroy its power. But the King of Men falters and decides against all that has been agreed and decides to keep the ring for himself. The Elvin Lord is at his side on the brink of the volcano's mouth and urges the king to adhere to the original agreement. He witnesses this change and through his grimy, battle-strained, sweat-covered face, the disbelief, the disappointment, the sheer frustration becomes visible.

"This scene is etched on my mind, frozen in time. The look upon his face (it's the same Australian actor who plays the Agent in the film The Matrix) is one I identify with. Battling so hard, risking life and limb, forming alliances, united in struggling against a common evil, only to be cruelly let down at the crucial moment. What trust can be formed following such a devastating betrayal?

"The other thing, which is running through my mind in close parallel, is being gunned down in no man's land. In my most vulnerable of states, reaching out for help only to have the person I am attempting to approach, turn on me, gun me down. In my mind, she shows no pity for my state. I hate her cruelty, her laughter at my distress. I feel betrayed, never dare trust so willingly again, be suspicious of her. Fucking bitch. Whore. Die in hell. I'll never let you hurt me again."

In the email Mac was firstly alluding to his negative experience with his mother in trying to help her from his father's violence and, secondly, to the time he stood up to his father.

Following this brave, courageous act of speaking out and protecting his mother, his parents acted normally around him and he was astounded that no one noticed. It took a supreme effort of will and courage for him to face the terror of his father. No-one noticed his need afterwards to be held and reassured. That was what he meant when he talked of being left in 'no man's land'.

His mum needed him desperately but she could never meet any of his needs. That was terrifying to the lonely Mac. Once again she was not there for him. She had not noticed him.

Fear of silence

Mac came today looking very disturbed and uncomfortable. After a while, he said, "Fuck it, I find it so difficult to be in groups." He paused, thought, and then said, "And in one to one sessions really, when I think about it."

"Can you say what it is you find so difficult?"

He paused for a while and then said, "I cannot deal with the silences."

"What happens?"

"I feel a massive pressure to end the silence."

"Why is it so important to end the silence?"

"Because I panic. It's desperation to find something to talk about and, if I can't, it creates panic."

"Do you share with anybody how you feel? With close friends?"

"I have done this with a couple of them, but it doesn't help."

"It doesn't help at all?"

"Not at all."

Inside I could feel the sense of being stuck and panic and the sense of not knowing what to do arising in me. It was clearly the experience that Mac had.

Mac then continued quite loudly, "I feel trapped 'lost, like there's no way out'."

"And then what happens?"

"I feel so stifled, so inhibited. I cannot wait to remove myself from that situation. I walk away."

"Mac," I said, grabbing a piece of paper and a pen, "let's observe and track your process around silence step by step and I'll write it down."

Mac gave me a look as if to say, 'how is that going to help?'

"OK. If we write down your process, you'll be able to witness it, observe it, and see how it happens, step by step, from a different perspective. That's its value and I'll give you the paper afterwards."

Mac nodded his head in agreement.

"First, Mac, you experience silence in a conversation. I want you to really put yourself in a situation and tell me what happens next."

"...Pressure to end the silence."

"Anything else?"

"If I'm asked to do something, I ascribe a gravity to it that's completely out of proportion."

"How does that make you feel?"

"Crushed. My heart starts sinking. I'm going to be disappointed."

He paused for a while looking like a little boy, very scared, then continued, "I feel powerless." His voice now sounded very young. "Scared that I can't..." He stopped in mid-sentence, eyes starting to blink rapidly, face flinching and contorting.

"... Wanting the violence to end. Not being able to escape that situation."

"Carry on, Mac. "I know it's difficult."

"Acute physiology of fear and suspicion, refusing to comply with what's being asked of me."

"Anything more?"

"I'm paralysed inside, frightened to move."

"This is obviously bringing up all that happened in your childhood."

"Yes," he said in a whisper, as if we shouldn't be heard.

"Mac, can you remember what happened prior to one of your dad's violent outbursts?"

He cringed a bit as he took himself back there. Then a flash of insight passed across his face. "Yes," he said a little excited, "there was a strange quietness and I always knew he was going to explode by that strange quietness, before it happened."

"Mac, could we say silence, that strange silence?"

"Yes," he nodded as he took in the memory of that silence.

"Mac, I'm wondering, if you interpret all silences now like you did when you were a little boy, whether silence equals violence."

He started to go white and perspire slightly. "Fuck it! That's it!" Again he said, "That's it. Fuck it. I always knew when he was going to go."

"And now you interpret any kind of silence as the prelude to danger and violence."

He looked astonished in the realisation of the unconscious effects of his trauma and the legacy and difficulty it had left him with in relationships.

Mac sat back, kind of relaxed. After giving him some space I asked him how he felt.

"Like a clean piece of Ikea pine."

"Is that good or bad?"

"Oh, good." He mumbled almost as if he didn't want to say it. Sometimes with Mac getting information was like pulling teeth.

A question of power

Mac sat there today with a snarl on his face. The bag that had been fitted because of my tumour grumbled and made various noises. Mac looked at me very sternly and pointed to that part of me. "What's it doing when it does that?" he asked in a very irritated fashion.

I said, "I will tell you, but I'm very interested to know what you will get from knowing?"

Mac just looked at me in a very surly manner. "I just

want to know!"

"But what will it give you to know Mac?"

Mac clinched his right fist, leaned forward and said to me in the coldest way, "I want to see you squirm."

"OK, what will it give you to see me squirm?"

Mac exploded, "I want to break your fucking confidence. You're so fucking confident as you sit there."

"So you break my confidence, Mac, what does that give you?"

"I would be on top."

"So, it's a question of power in this relationship?"

"Yes," he said vehemently.

He went very quiet and after a while looked up and said, "Why do I do that sort of thing? How can I be so cruel?"

"Because that part of your dad and his cruelty you experienced is what you are now capable of doing to others."

"But I don't want to."

"But you do and that's what you just did. It's better to invite that part of yourself into the room and start to accept that you can be cruel. We will work with it in our relationship, rather than deny it and have it explode and be out of your control."

Mac looked at me and said, "I want to cry."

"This saying has just come to me, Mac, and I'm going to tell you what it is. When Jesus was on the cross and he was being cruelly persecuted and tortured he said, 'Forgive them, they know not what they do'. And now, Mac, you do know what you do. Unlike the people in Jesus' time, you now start to have a choice about whether you keep on doing it."

This was a most amazing experience with Mac's cruelty. When he left I'd never felt so good – so completely whole, safe and strong. I was surprised that there was no anger. In fact, it felt like I had been given a gift somehow in Mac's showing me my own strength to deal with my experience of cancer. Since that session, this feeling has never left me. So in a strange way I am grateful to Mac, which I am sure would astound him. However, I don't see myself telling him!

Star Wars and Darth Vader

Mac came today. He didn't look his usual smart self. It was as if he wasn't looking after himself. He came in quietly and sat down for a while, carrying on from the end of our last session where he had become quite aggressive with me. He leaned forward, chin jutting out and snarled at me.

"You're not going to change me." He looked at me challengingly and confrontationally.

"Do you think I want to?"

He nodded to himself.

"No, you want to change. That is why you come here."

What I was working with was showing Mac how he bullies others and parts of himself. Mac sat there. "Could you go inside Mac?" I asked, as he has a good facility for imagery.

Mac quietly went inside. His face moved with pain. "There's a wax figure melting," he said, breathing faster. "I'm trying to hold it, to pick up the pieces, stop them melting, but as they melt they are running on the floor, going down the drain."

Surprisingly, Mac who doesn't cry very often started crying in deep despair. "As it was going down the drain I felt helpless that I couldn't stop it."

He waited a while and looked quite frightened. "I feel as if I'm engulfed in black swirling darkness down this drain. Terror deeper and deeper. It's a terrifying abuse." Mac now cried out, "Will he come, will he come, the guardian angel?" He paused, crying, "Will he come? The knight on the white charger, will he rescue me?"

Then he collapsed into the chair with the slow realisation that nobody had come to rescue him. As he sat there in utter aloneness, despair and resignation, I had been holding my breath. As I let go of my breath, my chest wheezed. Mac, to my amazement, smiled and looked comforted. His eyes moved as if he were following something.

He stared into my eyes with a look that was soft and warm. "When you wheezed just now it reminded me of Sandy."

"Sandy?"

"Sandy, my dog. He always used to make that noise when he lay down and stretched out. I find that very comforting."

It's very mysterious how the unconscious works sometimes. Suddenly Mac's inner image changed to what he described as 'a house out on the flatlands like in America'. At the same time, he said, the song by the Pussy Cat Dolls called *Don't you wish your girlfriend was hot like me?* was going through his mind. As Mac looked at the house a wind was roaring through it.

I asked, "Is it vacuuming the dust of distress?"

Mac smiled, nodded. "Yes, a spring clean." He looked comfortable for a while before his face clouded over. "There's a room I've never been in. It's at the top of the house."

"Can you go in?" I gently guided.

"I'm frightened." After a pause, he went in and shuddered. "It's like a psycho's house. A house of pain and cruelty. It's so dark." He paused again; his face had gone quite white. Then he said, "It's like Darth Vader."

"Can you just look at him, Mac?" I asked and felt what he felt.

Suddenly Mac looked relieved. "It's all changed. It's exactly like the scene at the end of *Star Wars*, where Darth Vader is no longer himself. He is Anakin now, about 60 years old.

"I keep hearing these words, 'an absence of threat, an absence of threat'." Mac's face looked profoundly relieved and curious.

After a long pause, in a tone with an expression of someone who finds the answer to something troubling him deeply, he said, "That's it – that's what she represents. No threat. An absence of threat."

"Are you referring to your girlfriend Lara?"

"Yes." He smiled the gentlest smile I've seen from him.

This was a most important moment as it was his first ever experience of not being under threat. His whole early life had been lived in an atmosphere of terror, of real and impending violence with no escape. He had never known anything else until this wonderful magical moment that his girlfriend, the first he had ever lived with, so transformatively represented.

While he reacted with titanic rage, irritation and claustrophobic tension to the inadequacies and behaviour of Lara that so disturbed him, he loved her. Now he knew why. She had given him the greatest gift of his life, an absence of threat.

"Mac," I said after I had allowed him the time to savour this marvellous moment, "what's happened?"

"The Pussy Cat Dolls are still singing."

"Does it connect with you at all?" I asked this because I knew the song *Don't you wish your girlfriend was hot like me?* had been haunting Mac and disturbing him until now. In fact he now knew he didn't wish his girlfriend to be a lot like the song. She'd given him the absence of threat.

As Mac sat there he said, "My image of the Darth Vader family portrait has come up again."

"Can you look at Darth Vader? Anakin as he is now. Can you look at Anakin?"

"Yes."

"Can you enter Anakin? Become him?"

Mac said that if he moved near him in his imagination, he was drawn to his eyes, but when he looked they were very powerful, like a black hole. He was frightened to enter and become Anakin.

"I know it's frightening but I'm here. See what happens if you can."

"The eyes are black: they are drawing me in." He went in and his voice became small like a little boy's. "Its like a huge black cave in here. Absolutely black."

"It's OK, Mac, I'm here."

Suddenly he looked relieved. "There are diamonds in the

ceiling and everywhere – it's like a starry night." Then he started to cry, really sob, tears running down his cheeks as he exclaimed, "This is too good for me, this is too good for me."

I think the experience of absence with no threat and the sense of no tension and the beautiful picture was too much for Mac. He had never known any of this in his life.

He said Sandy was back, happily sniffing around, curious as always.

I connected this to Mac as I talked to him. "So Sandy is just happy and curious. Are you still anxious?"

"Yes it's all great but there is something else now, I just feel angry. I just feel angry." Once again he looked forlorn.

"Can you have an attitude of embracing the anger too, so it's not an outsider? It's embraced, not abandoned? Last week when we worked with your anger, we discussed how tired it was, how weary it was."

Mac did this and then calmed right down, very still and just said in a whisper, "Diamonds in the dark, diamonds in the dark."

As he settled down, I looked at the clock and saw we had about ten minutes to go. It seemed a much longer journey. Mac's very powerful imagination can be used for his healing but if there are frightening images, he gets extremely scared. As he started to gently come back into the room, into the here and now, he looked at me and said, "It was a very powerful session last week and, when I went, it seemed to affect Lara. I think she will go for therapy and that's helpful.

"As you start to change inside, it will affect the dynamics of your relationship."

He told me she had cried a lot when he had met her last week and told him things she'd never spoken of before about being bullied.

As it came to the end of the session, the room felt quiet and warm and Mac looked across to me, staring straight into my eyes with the softest smile. "Thank you, thank you Bernie."

As he slowly left, I came back into the room which was quiet and warm. It seemed that the softest smile could permeate the room. "Amen, our Father," I started saying quite quietly. Something important just happened here.

Ready to let go

Unfortunately about this time I had to go in for my final operation. I was in hospital for about a month and expected to be unable to work for at least for four to six weeks. Previously, I had explained to Mac that that I would be unavailable for a time and that if he needed to find another therapist I would understand. But after that period Mac came back and we had a good few sessions together. He seemed much better for the break and had been able to integrate a lot of the work we had done together.

Now on his own, he had gained more confidence in dealing with the emotional issues he had experienced. But there was one significant change. Mac's relationship seemed to be very healthy for him and he was receiving much support so he decided to end therapy with the proviso that he could always come back.

FOOTNOTE

1   *Uber die Grundlage der Moral*, essay by German philosopher Arthur
    Schopenhauer, 1839.

Case Notes

✍ All relationships for Mac were emotionally filtered through the lens of a major trauma. That trauma was two fold. First there was the supreme effort of will and courage it had taken for Mac to face the terror of his father to protect his mother. Second he had suffered the terror of being completely abandoned by his mother at the very time he most needed her.

✍ This meant Mac found it incredibly difficult to trust anyone to be there for him. He feared that if he opened up to them and really needed them they would abandon him at his most vulnerable like his mother had done. He also feared he would be unable to get back from that level of vulnerability if he were to be abandoned. So, he concluded it was best not to be open or vulnerable. As he put it, if he were so vulnerable and abandoned he would feel as if he were caught between enemy bullets being fired at him in 'no man's land', like being in the First World War. It was life or death for him.

✍ Mac experienced many moments from films as meaningful metaphors. Sometimes they served as catalysts for bringing to the surface repressed emotions he had previously been unaware of but needed to express.

✍ *Watership Down* was incredibly helpful to him in many ways and on many levels. He identified with Bigwig's courage and concern and sacrifice for others. It acted as a mirror to his own confrontation with his dad. He also felt a huge sense of liberation as he shared Bigwig's emotion. The power, the beneficial therapeutic effect that this had on

Mac, cannot be overestimated. We returned to it many times and it echoed throughout his therapy.

✍ Working with Mac on *The Lord of the Rings* I was able to use Wormtongue as a metaphor for Mac's inner voice so that Mac became aware of it and of how it undermined him. Most importantly he became conscious of its whispering subtlety and its power to bring on dark moods of depression and aggression. He saw how Wormtongue's dominance over the King left the King in a sickly, feeble trance, manipulated and unable to govern. All this was very helpful for Mac because he was able to observe it from a third person perspective.

✍ In watching *The Lord of the Rings* Mac saw the dynamics of inner parts of himself as the genesis of much of the conflict he felt. One of the reasons that the film helped Mac so much was that its genius for imagery appealed to his artistic ability and rich imagination.

Pennie

After graduating, Pennie joined a London-based banking recruitment firm. Today she is an actress, due in no small way to the impact that one particular film had on her life.

Pennie chose for her session Life is Beautiful, a film in which she found the quality of acting to be 'quite extraordinary'. Life is Beautiful is based on a father/son relationship and their plight in a concentration camp. Such was the impact of the movie on Pennie that she left her job to take up acting, performing in an outdoor Shakespeare tour for three months before going on to pursue a career in theatre.

For Pennie, what was important about Life is Beautiful was the father's display of imagination used to shield his son from the terrifying circumstances in which they found themselves. He showed a level of love and positive influence that Pennie found in the relationship with her own father. In her own words, Life is Beautiful demonstrated and deepened her understanding of 'the value of how important children are'.

It emerged from our session that Pennie now saw some movies as being inspirational, particularly European films. "We all need a bit of inspiration — help with subtle changes in our lives."

Pennie found that talking about the film Life is Beautiful in the session had a calming effect on her. The session also gave her an insight into how potentially beneficial it would be to show movies in schools — on topics such as anorexia, for example. "Films engage you and I can't see how a film on such a topic wouldn't affect the audience. Younger people would respond to it — it's their world."

Talking about her experience and decisions she has made reconfirmed for Pennie that having meaning in her life was more important than anything else.

Maureen

Maureen conducted her life at breakneck speed to cover up her constant anxiety and depression. Because of what had happened to her as a child she felt dirty and ashamed. Her belief that she was never good enough and her fear of trusting people dogged her relationships. The television programme Celebrity Blind Man's Buff allowed her to remove the emotional blindfold that stopped her grieving for her dead father. Through the film The Bridges of Madison County she came to see how and why she had allowed the only man she loved to slip through her fingers.

Maureen had been referred to me by an alternative therapist. With her blue eyes, good features and thick brown-auburn hair she was a striking woman – and one with a very strong presence. She later chose the pseudonym 'Maureen' for herself as she bears a close resemblance to the actress Maureen Lipman in her appearance, expressions and sure-fire delivery.

Maureen looked at the cushions in the room and the chairs. "Where should I sit?" she asked in a chirpy voice.

"Wherever you want," I said. Maureen sat in an armchair.

"How can I help?"

Maureen looked at me and smiled. "I just don't have any confidence. I just lack confidence." She spoke these short staccato sentences very quickly. Her eyes darted about as she checked her bag and took a tissue. It seemed she was always doing something.

"Can you tell me about your life Maureen?"

"Oh, I don't know where to start really."

"Well, what was it like at home?"

"Always had an open house. My aunt stayed at weekends, and my cousin with three kids. I had holidays with cousins. It was a happy time. I remember my aunt having a nervous breakdown, and I would see her sometimes rocking in a chair." She paused.

I wasn't sure whether Maureen was being consciously or unconsciously funny about having a lovely time while her aunt was rocking in the corner having a nervous breakdown. This was to happen many times in our sessions. Sometimes she was intentionally funny, sometimes unconsciously funny, but I had to remind myself not to let it distract me from the serious work we were doing together.

"At school I didn't always feel part of the group. I was always trying but I did not want to play up and get into trouble."

"Maureen," I asked, "do you mean that to be accepted by the group you would have had to do things that meant you would get into trouble?"

"Yes," she said, "I was afraid of a telling off from my mum." Her brow furrowed and she looked quite anxious. Then she said with a sigh, "I was also afraid of being a goody-goody."

I said, "It feels to me like you couldn't win."

She nodded quickly, her blue eyes radiating her pleasure at being understood.

"Maureen, can you tell me more about being good?"

"Oh yes, I had to be good when my mum took me to work with her. I always had to be quiet as she worked as a cleaner in posh people's houses." She stopped and went silent.

In this pause, while I allowed Maureen some space and some silence, I became aware of a sense of tension. Maureen moved continuously while she was thinking.

"I don't know what else to say."

"Well," I encouraged her, "anything else that comes to you about what it was like in those years, just for me to get some sense of your history."

"Dancing. My mum used to take me to dancing classes and I always felt I had to be good, always trying to get everything right. Had to do well in exams, shows and competitions. I am always looking for praise."

"OK, who's not?"

"At parties, I was quiet and shy. I wanted to join in but I was so frightened of being rejected, made a fool of, and humiliated."

"Had you been humiliated at all?" I asked.

Maureen thought for a while and then said, "In the dance class my mum always compared me to Suzie, another dancer, like she got it right and I got it wrong. And when the teacher shouted at me I couldn't take anything in. I just felt thick. I was confident at home in family situations – happy and relaxed. Sometimes I feel like the snobby cousin. I try not to be looking down my nose at anyone, but I'm embarrassed by them."

Maureen thought again for a while, then was distracted by the rain on the window. Unconsciously, even though there was still more time left, she reached for her umbrella saying, "I hope I've got it with me, I don't want to get drenched. Oh yes, there it is." This pattern of being distracted by events inside or outside the room would often happen in subsequent sessions. It was very difficult to keep Maureen on one particular subject or focused inside herself.

Maureen continued, "When I was at secondary school

my friends were going to pubs and clubs. I didn't because my mum, who always worried about how I'd get home, never wanted me to be out. I felt that I was missing out on life, fun, jokes, relationships." Maureen looked really sad at this point. "My best friend turned against me. I can't remember why she wanted to pick a fight with me but I wouldn't fight. I tried to but then all the friends turned against me and I felt alone again. I was not comfortable being naughty or being good."

I glanced at the clock. Our time had gone very fast. I wanted to inform Maureen of my session ending procedure, about how I always tell my clients when there is 10 minutes to go so they can prepare for the outside world. Also, I always ask, 'how has the session left you?' because if clients haven't had therapy before, they are looking to the therapist for guidance on how it's done.

When I asked Maureen how the session had left her, she replied, "Well, I don't feel any better." (She gave me a sidelong glance that was comical and judgemental all in one.)

"Did you expect to in the first session?"

"Well I'd hoped to, don't know really" she said quickly, a bit defensively.

Realising her impatience I said, "Well, it won't be quick. We need time to get to know one another – to see if we both feel we could continue to work together. I do feel I could work with you."

"Oh good." Maureen said very quickly and laughed. "Yes," she added, "yes."

"Sorry Maureen, yes what?"

She looked at me as if I was dim. "Yes, I could continue to work with you. Yes, I feel OK with you."

"Fine."

Maureen grabbed her umbrella and coat, leaving with a throw-away comment, "I'll see you next week, if I don't get carried away by the flood."

With that she was gone. My feeling was that she was a nice person but there was something I couldn't put my finger on. I also realised her fast pace, sharpness of mind and constant hopping from one subject to another demanded that I remain grounded and very aware in our sessions.

Fear of getting things wrong

Maureen breezed in, very efficient and then asked for a glass of water. "I get very dry," she explained, "I have this condition."

"Yes, I'll get you one." I observed, very surprised, that I was doing this. I was a therapist and very seldom did I wait on clients with cups of tea or water!

"Thank you," Maureen said.

While taking a few gulps of water she talked about how very hot and stuffy the tube had been and how she had been worried about not getting to me on time. Then she looked blankly at me, waved her hand and said, "Come on, come on." I realised I was being organised to ask her questions.

I sat there, quite surprised really, and thought about the situation for a moment. If I complied, I was accepting her control and if I didn't she would be totally stuck and feel awkward. As these were early sessions where the relationship needs to be built and the client has to develop a sense of safety and trust, I decided to comply.

"Well, how are you feeling now?"

"OK," she said flatly, looking at me rather incredulously, like somehow that wasn't the right question.

"Any sensation in your body?"

Maureen now looked appalled. "I have pins and needles in my arm, if that's what you mean!" There was more than a little sarcasm in her voice. I could see she was still processing that question by the look of puzzlement that crossed her face.

Early sessions of therapy can take on an educative quality in parts. So I continued to explain my question. "The reason I am asking about sensations in your body is that we often have repressed feelings which manifest themselves physically. So when you start to feel them, connect with them, you may or may not start to have some memories, which would be helpful."

Maureen's response really amused me. "Righty-oh then." She checked her body for a split second with an air of 'OK I'll play this game if you want.' "Well, nothing. Nothing there at all." She looked at me challengingly. I stayed quiet. Maureen then began drumming her fingers impatiently and said, "Come on, come on," her right hand beckoning me. I sat there astounded. It was clear that Maureen liked being in control.

"Maureen, I notice that any time you've answered a question and there is a silence you beckon me very quickly to ask more questions."

Before I could say any more, Maureen said, "I can't bear silences, can't bear them. Never could."

"Really, tell me about that, what is it about them?"

Almost as the last word had left my mouth, Maureen replied, "Don't know, just don't like them." Then came the challenging look again.

"Maureen, that response was too quick. I need you to take some time to go inside yourself and think. Let us try to slow this right down."

Maureen looked a little hurt. "Well, I've never done this before." Her tone sounded as if she felt I was criticising her.

"Maureen, how did you just experience my asking you to slow it down?"

She looked uncomfortable again. "Well, like I was getting it wrong. That's how my mum would treat me."

"Ah," I said, "so you are experiencing me like your mum?"

"Yes," she said, looking angrily at me. "She did that all the time."

"Well, Maureen, that is very interesting but I want you to know that I'm not criticising you and I wonder if you experience that feeling of irritation and of being criticised with other people in your life?"

"Yes," she said, looking more thoughtful. "I do with some bosses or some friends."

"So you're not experiencing them as them but as your mum?"

"Yes, I suppose I am." She went quiet for a while and was thoughtful. "I just don't know what to do."

"No, I know," I said gently, "and I'll show you. But any time you feel that I'm criticising you I want you to tell me directly."

"OK," said Maureen smiling, with a look that said 'I like that, and boy am I going to keep you to it!'

"Maureen, why you don't like silences?"

"They just make me feel uncomfortable – tense and awkward."

"When's the first time you remember feeling like that?"

"I've always felt like that, for as long as I can remember."

"And you have no idea why?" Maureen shifted around in her chair, looked very uncomfortable and said with irritation, "I don't know what to do. I just don't know what to do. I don't know what's expected of me."

"So my sense is that you are lost and that you feel threatened in some way?"

Maureen then had a memory from her childhood. "I remember when I used to do my homework, often my mum would hover about me silently and suddenly she would shout, 'Have you done this? Have you done that?' in a critical, agitated fashion and that made me feel nervous and very unsure of myself. I would freeze – couldn't think at all. My mind just stopped. Then my mum would get even more agitated as though I was thick."

"So it seems you are connecting that memory with how you feel about silences?"

"Yes," said Maureen quietly.

The room felt quite still with an atmosphere like something

had just been completed. I felt quite pleased that Maureen was making these connections and I was beginning to see her patterns of transference in our sessions – as witnessed in her hearing me criticise her when I wasn't.

I glanced at the clock. "We are coming to the end now. How has the session left you feeling?"

"Not sure," she said, "but something's happened inside me."

"Is it good, bad or neutral?"

"Oh, good," said Maureen, looking at me with great surprise as if I should know. "Well," she said looking at her watch and hurriedly getting her things together, "I must get on as I'm meeting my friends and I'll probably be late. Anyway I'll just tell them I was with my psycho. "Bye," she said in a cheery voice and was gone.

Her psycho? I was left with the words ringing in my ears. What does she mean, psycho? It felt like a put down. I would have to ask her in the next session.

Hidden feelings

Rat-a-tat on the door. "Hi ya." Maureen comes straight in like a whirlwind. "Can I use your loo? I've been sitting on that train and it was boiling hot. Oh, and can I have a glass of water?" I felt very amused at all of this, dutifully got her a glass of water and waited for her to come back.

Maureen sat down, looked at me expectantly. I just waited a while quietly. "Come on, come on," she said.

"Maureen, is there anything you feel you want to say?

Or, do you have to wait for me to ask you a question?"

"No. But you're the therapist." She said looking at me challengingly with a mixture of humour and deadly seriousness.

No room for waffle here I thought! I sat there feeling stuck. After a while I asked, "How did you feel after your last session?"

"Good. OK. But afterwards, when I was with my friends, I also felt uncomfortable from things that had come up in the session."

"What made you feel uncomfortable?"

"All those memories."

"Any one in particular?"

"Well, about being critcised. And I realised that I like being in groups."

"Did you feel uncomfortable with any of your friends?"

"Not really," said Maureen quickly, "just from the session." Then she said on reflection "Oh yes, there is one. Sarah makes me feel uncomfortable sometimes."

"Uncomfortable. Do you mean criticised?"

"Yes."

"So you experience Sarah like your mum as well."

Maureen looked quite pleased. "Yes, I suppose I do. I've never looked at it like that."

Maureen sat quietly for a bit. Interestingly, she was not affected by the silence this time, obviously because she was thinking and wasn't putting any pressure on herself to perform. It seemed that when she was thinking she was unaware and undisturbed by the silence but then, in relating to someone, she felt uncomfortable and uncertain what to do.

Maureen suddenly said, "I told my friends I had been to see you, my psycho, and they asked why I called you that."

"Yes, why do you?"

"Well it's just a kind of a joke."

"But I don't quite understand, what do you mean?"

Maureen thought for a minute. "Well it's like when people ask where my dad is or refer to him. I just say 'well he's up there playing on his harp, I suppose'."

I thought to myself: so this is the way that Maureen deals with strong feelings. The explanation about her dad being on his harp seems almost a put-down, quite sharp when she says it. She speaks in such a throw away manner about something so important as if it doesn't matter. So is it difficult for Maureen to connect with her real feelings about her dad being dead and how she feels about me in her life. Her throw away attitude as she speaks is one I will continue to observe more closely and in particular I will take note of what we are talking about when she does it.

There is something about the times when she does this that is important. The joke doesn't work somehow. It throws the other person. What I am left with is a vague feeling of unease and lack of connection and I'm wondering if this is the cost to Maureen in her way of dealing with these very sensitive issues. In fact she cuts herself off from the very heart to heart connection she so yearns for, for nurture in her life.

Maureen continued, "In my teens, when I was socialising, I was on the outskirts of a group yet again. I felt unsure but never let my feelings show. I felt vulnerable and scared of losing my friends."

She explained that she had also found herself uncertain in male company – unsure of what was expected of her. "I didn't know how to react, lacked confidence and conversation."

Maureen suddenly brightened up. "When I was older, I felt comfortable and relaxed with a horny married boss. I'd known him for three years before our relationship started. We were very happy most of the time. He'd separated from his wife and…" she broke off and went silent. Suddenly she looked angry and sad and started pulling at the thread of the cushion. "I got so upset when he two timed me, extremely upset when he returned to his wife without telling me." She went very, very quiet, unusually so for Maureen.

"How did that make you feel?"

Maureen was silent for a while and then she said, "I felt hurt." There was a long pause. "…and betrayed. I couldn't eat. I tried to eat sometimes but it just made me sick. I threatened to walk in front of a bus once when I was drunk."

Then she straightened herself up. "C'est la vie."

She made it clear that she didn't want to talk anymore about that. I didn't persist but thought I would come back to it another time. There are times to be firm and times to go easy as a therapist and at this particular moment I felt it was best to go easy, but it was a clear indication of how bad she felt.

Maureen continued. "I then met Richard. I was very comfortable with him, but not sharing all feelings for fear of saying too much, especially the second time."

"Do you mean that you broke off and went back with him?"

"Oh yes, he's a friend now, but this has gone on and off for years."

"So what were you afraid of the second time?"

"That we would get too close and I would get hurt." Maureen now looked very angry and hurt clouded her face. "I was really upset when he went back to his previous girlfriend without telling me. I loved his company. He always made me laugh."

"So once again, Maureen, I'm hearing that another man you were very fond of has returned to a previous partner, but not told you."

"Yes," she said in a kind of miles-away fashion. Then she continued, "With Richard I felt I would go for it; let go of any feelings of holding back, being hurt and scared except when asked about relationships. I felt I was not worthy or worldly, had not had many experiences. I felt towards the end of this relationship that I was trying to please him. I thought I could change him, but I couldn't. I wonder if it's because I felt dirty."

I realised it was 6.55pm and felt so frustrated because Maureen was opening up on something very powerful and new. "Maureen, we are coming to the end now and I'd very much like to pick up on what made you feel dirty in our next session."

She jumped up, very quickly and said, "Okey dokey."

"Not so fast, Maureen, just check and see how the session leaves you."

"Alright," she said in a very matter of fact way, "not cured but alright." She gave me a teasing smile and was gone.

I wandered back into the session room intrigued by what appeared to be a pattern of Maureen choosing men who were already committed to someone else. Was the fact that she picked men who are not really available an indication of her own ambivalence towards commitment I wondered.

Feeling dirty

Maureen arrived in her usual rush. "Can I use your loo?" she asked as she put down her coat and handbag.

"Yes, OK." Bang, bang, bang up the stairs.

When Maureen returned, she sat down and exhaled. "Phew."

"I had a really busy day today." Then she glanced at her hand and I saw she was crossing her fingers as if to remind herself. "I've got something to tell you," she said very quickly, "but I'll tell you later."

She glanced at my hand and saw a bruise on it. "Do you want some arnica on that?"

"No thank you Maureen," I replied smiling.

"I always do that: everyone treats me like I'm a nurse."

"That's very kind of you, but here is where I look after you."

"Oh," she said blushing, looked down and said quietly, "Thank you."

"Maureen, at the end of last week's session, something important came up about your feeling dirty. Could you tell me how that happened and when it started?"

"Yes, feeling dirty."

"One day," Maureen said, "I was with a couple of little boys, the same age as me. We were six years old and we were looking at each others' genitals innocently, just curious, you know. Suddenly my mum came round the corner and caught us." The colour drained from Maureen's face as she re-lived that moment. "I will never, ever forget the look upon her face. I felt so terrible, so dirty, it's never left me. My mum just said, 'Maureen, come with me immediately'.She was very angry and I felt I just wanted to curl up and die. I really felt ashamed."

"But, Maureen," I said, "when we look at it now, can you accept that you were only a little girl doing what is purely natural, out of a healthy curiosity?"

"I know, but I still feel dirty sometimes."

"Well the more we talk about it, get it out in the open, your feelings about it will gradually dissolve."

"I hope so," Maureen said, "as I was very confused around men. My mother made me so cautious around men when I was going through my teenage years."

"How did she do that?"

"Well, all she kept repeating was that men were only after one thing. I think she was terrified of me coming home pregnant."

"Are you saying to me that you connected those feelings of being dirty and of men being only after one thing?"

Maureen was silent for a while and then said, "Yes. I don't know what men want or how to be and whether to trust them or not." She paused and then said slowly like an insight was coming to her, "Maybe it's also because my dad died so young that I don't know how to be around men."

"Well, Maureen, I think you're right. That really is a contributing factor."

Maureen was now crying. "She makes me furious. I am a 40 year-old woman yet here I am still affected by the sense of shame which that moment brought up in me." Maureen took tissue after tissue angrily, wiped her eyes and nose and then looked at me. "I am going to get all clogged up now. I always do when I cry." She shook her head vigorously from side to side. Her voice was now like a little girl's.

"I think it's very good that you are expressing feelings that have been buried for all these years."

Maureen gazed into the distance looking very sad then gradually said, "I feel a bit easier now."

"How do you mean? Can you tell me if it has affected your body in any way?"

Maureen waited a moment, checked and then pointed to her chest. "Here. I feel I can breathe more easily, like a weight has gone."

"Good," I said.

The session was now coming to a close. We both look at her crossed fingers. She said, "I can't remember what I wanted to tell you...C'est la vie!" Then she asked, "Is it time?"

"Yes."

"OK, I'm going home to see my mum now, grrrrrrr!" She did an imaginary strangling of her mum with her hands. It was very good that she now found it easier to express her anger and frustration with her mother in our sessions and she unconsciously could be very funny at these times too – but not every time. Sometimes there was just black rage with no humour.

Taking things literally

Maureen turned up at one particular session and said very matter of factly, as if ordering a coffee, "Oh, by the way, I've got to have a heart valve replaced. They are talking about maybe using a pig's heart valve, but I don't know yet."

"When's this?" I asked, surprised and struck by the seriousness of the situation.

"Oh, in about three months, I think," she said airily. "They told me I would feel much better afterwards."

I was shocked. As Maureen continued at breakneck pace I asked myself how she could not have mentioned something so important before.

"Maureen, can we pause a moment? This is very important and this is the first I have heard anything about it."

Maureen gave me a look as if to say 'come on doc, pull yourself together'.

I said, "It's important that we talk about how you feel about this."

"Oh well, if it's got to be done, it's got to be done and if I feel better for it… Sometimes I get out of breath going up stairs and escalators and all that."

I was concerned for the level of anxiety she lived with in her life and how she drove herself. Now there was the news of this heart condition. I wondered about the break-neck pace and throw away manner in which she had told me about the possible heart operation. Was it that she knew she had to tell me but really didn't want to talk about it? Maybe she thought that if she went at a fast pace she would bewilder me and, hopefully, I would not question her further about it so she would not have to examine her feelings.

Maureen subsequently had the operation. It was a success but not from her point of view because she did not seem to make any allowances for how weak she would feel as she recuperated and convalesced afterwards. Very angry and upset, she cried tearfully, "They told me I would be alright and I am not alright." Again, this showed two important things about Maureen: her lack of trust after her father's death and how she would take things literally. I came to understand how the latter could lead to bitter disappointment for her.

We dealt with these issues over many sessions during her year of recuperation.

In-tray, out-tray

Maureen arrived at this particular session in her usual everyday panic. She had no time to breathe and said as she walked up the passage, "I was so busy at work today; I'm just fed up with it. I've got so many things to talk to you about and oh, my mum is driving me mad."

Maureen sat down. Gulping down her glass of water, she said, "I am just so tired. I wake up early and can't stop thinking."

"Thinking about what?"

"Work really: I'm just not getting it together. I'm just not doing all the things I need to do to catch up." Maureen stopped for a brief moment. Inside, I was feeling concerned about how hard she was pushing herself after her heart operation which was surely adding to her exhaustion and depression.

Inside, I wondered how to proceed with Maureen's desire for comfort and contentment, which was quite plainly not available to her because of her obsessive thinking. There was no time to pause and breathe in her world – just busy, busy, busy, with an obsessive focus on her performance and the standard that she had to reach. The challenge was how to help her to become aware of this but in a way where she didn't feel criticised or not good enough.

I decided to talk to Maureen about her obsession with her in-tray in work and also in life and her lack of focus and attention on her out-tray in work and in life. She was always so focused on what she had to do that her life was one long journey and effort of doing. If she could start to see what she had achieved each day in work and in life this would redress the balance and the demands that she placed on herself. It would also lower the stress and pressure that came from those demands.

"Maureen, at work you seem to be obsessed with your in-tray, in other words with what you have to do. I want you to become just as obsessed with your out-tray because you never pay any attention to what you have achieved.

Maureen was looking at me with a quizzical eye but was also very interested. Suddenly, while I was still in full flow, she crossed her fingers and said, "I've got to tell you something in a minute." I managed to stay focused and carry on as Maureen grabbed her notebook and scribbled something down quickly. "OK, OK," she said, "I just had to remember that too."

I continued, "It's exactly the same one-sided focus you take to your whole life. In other words, you are obsessed with what you have to do but never look at what you've achieved, which leaves you in a constant state of anxiety and low self-esteem. If you were to look at what you have achieved as much as what you have to achieve you would be much calmer and have more self esteem."

Maureen looked at me unusually quietly and nodded. She seemed to have found a more contemplative mood than I had ever seen before. At the end of our session she got up just that little bit more slowly and said goodbye in a softer, less staccato and tense tone of voice. I felt quite pleased that something had shifted and very interested that Maureen had not mentioned what she had intended to tell me. This was a first!

Relationships that don't last

Maureen breezed in, drank her water with a gulp and said, "I went dancing at the weekend. I really enjoyed it but it makes me feel tired. Sometimes I can't do what I used to. Didn't meet any fellas though," she said making a face. "Ç'est la vie!"

"Maureen, do you really want a regular relationship?"

Maureen looked at me as if I'd just stepped off the moon. "Of course! But they just don't last. I have been out with different men but it's never lasted. I don't know why." With this Maureen looked at the floor and went quiet. She started twiddling with her rings. I tensed up inside. Any movement towards her rings was a signal for a diversion or something she wanted to tell me and I was ready for her notebook to suddenly appear for her to take down something she had to do when she left me.

"Maureen, I see you are touching your rings..."

Before I could say more Maureen said, "No wedding ring though." She looked at me challengingly. I immediately felt totally responsible for Maureen's dilemma.

I noted it and asked, "Do you feel it's something to do with you that you have not found someone to marry or that a relationship won't last?"

With the speed of light Maureen came back with, "Well I'm the one they leave."

I felt suitably chastised. "You seem quite angry."

"Yes, well I don't know what men want," she said crossing and uncrossing her legs at that moment, tears beginning to well up in her eyes. This physical uncrossing of her legs, I noted, brought to my mind her mother saying men only want one thing.

Celebrity Blind Man's Buff

Maureen turned up today in her usual rushed way, but there was an air of excitement about her. She began, "I watched this programme at the weekend. It opened up something that for years of counselling I could not visit with any depth. I watched it and amazingly it opened doors to my past."

I was very pleased. "What was the programme?" I asked.

"*Celebrity Blind Man's Buff*. Three celebrities, Sean Hughes, Linda Robson and Gail Porter were challenged to travel from Blackpool to London wearing blacked out glasses. They were on their own, though each had a silent personal guide and film crew. They had to use many different forms of transport separately and have an overnight stay in a hotel or B and B. Finally, each celebrity was met at a London station by a guide who was truly blind. This 'blind guide' helped them to their meeting point at the London Eye. Needless to say, all three celebrities learnt a lot. Not only was it interesting, but also amusing in places and very moving."

I sat there enthralled, as Maureen continued with her account of the programme.

"I found two instances where I became overwhelmed with Gail's emotional reaction. The first was when she 'trusted' a young lady to guide her from a shopping centre, only to find herself being guided into a concrete bollard." Maureen's eyes were gradually beginning to well up with tears. I noticed as well was how totally still she was whilst remembering this rather than being mobile all the time as usual.

Maureen went on, "The second instance was when, having reached the final destination, Gail was free to remove the blacked out glasses. This was a most dramatic moment as she flooded with tears at the realisation that she 'could take the glasses off' and see, unlike her guide who was totally blind."

I questioned Maureen further and after some time asked her what she thought Gail was feeling when she took the glasses off. She thought for a while before replying. "Gail was experiencing the combined emotional relief of taking the glasses off and realising that she could just walk away from the programme and continue her life, unlike her guide who could not walk away from his blindness."

"How did you feel watching this, Maureen?" I asked. "What was it that got to you?"

"I cried and felt great emotion."

"But do you know what that emotion was about?"

Maureen thought for a while, quickly grabbing her tissues. "I realised how in the dark I have felt surrounding the illness and death of my dad. Not knowing what was going on at that time."

As Maureen wept quietly, I gave her a bit of space to cry. After a while she continued, "I somehow felt he died because I was not good enough. I was told by my teacher that if I was a good girl everything would be alright and when he died I felt it was because I had been bad." Maureen sobbed as she realised the emotional impact this belief had made on her life.

After some time and space, she looked calmer and more serene in this new realisation that her Dad's death was nothing to do with her behaviour or with her not being good enough. The emotional relief she felt at the removal of the guilty burden she had carried since she was eight years old cannot be emphasised enough. She was in a state of quiet shock, still dazed when she left.

At the precise moment in *Celebrity Blind Man's Buff* that Gail Porter took the glasses off and could see, Maureen identified with her own blindness to her emotional past. She realised that unconsciously she had felt and seen everything in relation to her father.

Release from emotional blindness

Over the next few sessions I continued to look at how Maureen had felt since seeing *Celebrity Blind Man's Buff*. At the beginning of one particular session Maureen sat down thoughtfully and then said, "I think I've realised something else".

"What's that?"

Slowly she continued, "I've realised that my mum could not tell me the truth, because I don't think she could bear seeing me cry when she was so sad herself." Maureen cried quietly. She was gradually coming to terms with how she had seen things and was starting to understand her anger with her mother. Now that anger was beginning to change into some compassion for her mother's emotional predicament at the time as a grieving widow with a young daughter.

There was another development for Maureen. The little girl in her was annoyed that she had not been told the truth and had been kept in the dark about her dad's illness – even more so now. She said she felt she could have coped with the truth if her mother had been honest with her.

From the time of that experience on, Maureen had found it difficult to trust anybody but herself. What haunted her was the last memory of her dad waving to her from the hospital window. It was like she felt she had been cheated: not being able to sit on his bed in the hospital so he could hold her and kiss her.

Always trying to be good enough and feeling responsible for her dad's death, Maureen had been guilt ridden and driven to the point of exhaustion. Now she said she felt as if a weight had been lifted from her chest.

It was also important for Maureen to experience her physical feelings to *Celebrity Blind Man's Buff* as well as the repressed ones. I asked her what had moved her so much about Gail Porter removing her blindfold. Again she started to cry. She thought for a while and said, choking on her words, "It was her compassion, the fact...that she realised the real blind person could not take any blindfold off."

When Maureen first came to me she treated her emotions with a flippant jokey denial – never looking inside with any depth. Her answer, when anyone asked her about her father, was given in a cold, throwaway line 'ah, he's dead, probably up there playing his harp...' Now Maureen was able to free herself from her emotional blindness to her past.

As she continued to sob I said gently, "I wonder if the compassion you saw Gail Porter expressing touched the part of you that so much needed compassion around your dad's death and showed you the very compassion you have been unable to give to yourself?"

Maureen sat there, miles away for a period, then said through her tears, "I think you are right."

"Only your own feelings and experience will tell you."

I went on to explain that her inability to access that so needed compassion for herself for all these years had kept her in the dark about her father. Her emotional blindfold of denial had kept her from her healing compassion – from the completion of her grieving.

She needed to come to terms with how shocked and betrayed she had felt when being told by the teacher and her mother that everything would be OK if she was a good girl. She had interpreted this as her father would be fine. The sense of shock she experienced on realising she would never see him again had left her unable to trust anybody deeply.

The Bridges of Madison County

It was the evening when Maureen was due. There was cold, drizzling rain on the window. The phone rang. "Hi, hi, it's me," said a very out of breath Maureen. "I am at Gospel Oak station, train delayed, so I will be a bit late."

"OK, don't worry. Thanks for ringing."

I wanted to say *slow down*. The image of Maureen's heart valve scar flashed into my mind. *Don't strain yourself too much, Maureen*, I said to myself, realising at the same time this was not the right moment to address it with her. It would only serve to make her more stressed. I wondered how can we cut through this life or death intensity.

Maureen arrived breathless, talking very fast, cursing the tube, taking off her coat as she walked down the hallway, checking her rings. Then she flopped down into the armchair, with a long drawn out sigh of relief.

"Just take your time, Maureen, and let yourself arrive."

"Arrive! I thought it was never going to happen."

The period of Maureen's convalescence from the heart operation brought up many emotions for her when, at the same time, Richard, who moved in and out of her life, came on the scene again. It was always very jerky with Maureen. I could never get the full sense of the story of how she met Richard, so I decided to ask her.

Richard had been a consistent friend of Maureen over a number of years. He seemed to move in and out of her life when they met for the occasional meal together, or went to the odd dance or function where Maureen would be his escort. Maureen had known Richard before he was married and their friendship had continued through his marriage and subsequently through his divorce. Maureen underlined that she was not the reason for Richard's divorce.

Richard's wife at that time was a friend of Maureen's and was, coincidentally, called Maureen. She was also the same age. When Richard told her he was going to marry Maureen I asked her how she felt. "Oh, I felt very pleased for them both."

"Pleased!" I said quite surprised.

"Yes," she said, looking at me like a little girl who had done something wrong.

"Are you saying you only felt pleased for him and that was it?"

"Yes," she insisted defiantly. She went quiet as she reflected and then said slowly, "But when he left I took a shower and I burst out crying uncontrollably."

I sat there astounded, as Maureen had not connected these two things. She was not in touch with her feelings and could not get any further.

I smiled and continued, "Maureen, the *Celebrity Blind Man's Buff* experience was so beneficial I'd like to ask you, is there any other programme or film that has moved you in that way?"

"Oh yes," she said matter-of-factly, "*The Bridges of Madison County*." I sat there stunned as I had not heard any of this before.

In the film, the children of Francesca Johnson (Meryl Streep) are going through her possessions after her death. The discovery of her diary, love letters and various keepsakes enables the film to flash back to the mother's life and her intense, four-day love affair with a photographer Robert Kincaid (Clint Eastwood) who had drifted into town temporarily.

The film is about a woman torn between a very good, reliable husband and her romantic attraction and love for the photographer. Her dilemma about whether to stay with her husband leads to a crucial decision for her. She is a passionate but somewhat bored woman in this small town and her affair with the photographer changes her whole life.

The moment that Maureen identified with, and that made her sob in the cinema, was when the photographer turns and says, "I shall only say this once. This kind of certainty [the love they feel for one another] comes only once." It was at this point that Maureen realised she had let the only man she loved slip through her fingers.

As we continued with the session and as Maureen began to become aware of her powers of denial: I think she was somewhat stunned herself.

She had denied her feelings for Richard by constantly adjusting to what he wanted, never acknowledging how she felt and what she wanted, even to herself. She feared that if he got to know the real Maureen he would abandon her as she was not good enough. The Bridges of Madison County brought up the feelings of regret and sadness, of love and yearning, which she could no longer deny.

Maureen's role throughout the relationship with Richard had been like a confidante or secretary that he could sleep with. She organised their meetings, visits to the theatre and meals out together. She was purely reactive to his needs. Sometimes she would not see him for months on end and they would have no contact at all. When they did meet up, they might end up spending the night together, but not often.

This relationship was not about sex. For Maureen it was just about staying in contact with him. A little was better than nothing in her eyes.

Maureen continued to cry with regret over the wasted years of not declaring her love for Richard. Identifying totally with the dilemma of the Meryl Streep character in the film, Maureen realised that she had never made that choice — the choice being to acknowledge her love for Richard and to tell him.

It was the previous work we had done, of gradually showing her the cost of her denial, combined with the film, that cut through that denial so effectively. But it took subsequent sessions to connect it all in her emotional life.

When I later asked after she saw the film, "How do you feel about this other woman called Maureen, who got all that you wanted?" she started to cry.

"Sad." She cried more. "I suppose I just thought it would happen to me."

"Do you still love him?"

"Yes," she cried louder, "I probably do."

In subsequent sessions, what I found interesting was that this man had a history of failed relationships. But, as I pointed out to Maureen, their relationship was still going. I mused out loud that he'd had a pattern of choosing partners who were destined to fail, but by his not choosing her, she and he had stayed together. He did not mess it up.

Maureen looked at me like a little girl, wet eyes wide open, innocent as that possibility dawned on her. She too, because of losing her dad so early in her life, was living out this pattern. She was living out a distant relationship with a boyfriend who was not there like her distant relationship with her dad, a relationship from afar.

Putting the puzzle together

Over following sessions Maureen gradually put the fragments of her emotional life puzzle together and that process began in this session in response to my questions.

"I felt strong feelings as I had let the one person I truly loved slip through my fingers. I could not allow myself to be open with him for fear that if he knew the 'true' me, he would not love me."

"What was it about the real you that you were so concerned about?"

She sighed, thought for a moment, and then slowly said, "The memory of the childhood experience where my mum caught me with the boys. I felt such shame and disgrace and believed I was not worthy of love."

"Is there any other reason you feel that you would not be worthy of love?"

"Of course," she said sharply. "I was told if I was a good girl when my dad was ill everything would be alright. Well it wasn't."

"So does that mean that because your father died you think you were a bad girl and that his death was your fault?"

"Yes," she said looking dazed, "I suppose I do." Maureen at this moment was lost in thought at what she had just said.

I gave Maureen space as she sat there quietly, processing her reactions, considering the impact of those childhood beliefs on her life. After a pause she continued, "Also with my father dying when I was six years old, I had an inbuilt fear that anyone I loved would love and then leave me."

Once again Maureen paused to reflect on what she was saying.

"Do you think all those things are true now Maureen?"

Maureen smiled, looked at me and said quietly, "I didn't know I thought all those things. It's just coming out now." She looked very young when she spoke.

"Well, now as an adult with me in therapy you can trust the reality of those beliefs and understand how they've affected your life. Do you want to let go of some of them?"

Maureen's eyes were wet and soft and she sat there with a stillness and a peace that I had never seen before in our sessions.

Case Notes

🖋 Maureen's experiences of her mother constantly telling her to be quiet when she was doing her cleaning job, could have left her with a belief that it was wrong to be visible. 'Don't make a noise' could also have become a belief: 'Don't exist'. Things said consistently like this can be absorbed by a young mind into their unconscious and affect their personality in a negative way for the rest of their life – without their awareness. I contemplated the possibility that this belief could then have become, 'Don't be visible because when you are, you are ridiculed'.

🖋 It was very clear that Maureen must have been in conflict because she had a big personality and the desire to be seen. This, she was to tell me later, had affected her if she was in a group. She had no trouble getting the attention but, when she got it, she didn't know what to do with it and felt uncomfortable. That is when the beliefs 'don't be visible', and 'you have to get it right', reared themselves in her relationships.

🖋 What gradually emerged in our sessions were the experiences she had lived through as a child. She had connected those experiences together in an unconscious way that gave her a crippling negative core belief about herself. Maureen was deeply traumatised that she had done something wrong, that she was bad and that there was something wrong with her. This compounded her already established belief that she was not good enough. The innocent pre-adolescent curiosity and exploration of her genitals and the boys' was so shaming and disgraceful to Maureen, because of her mother's reaction. This reaction had compounded the belief that she was not worthy of love.

✍ Maureen would come in full of work-related problems. She would use the session predominantly to work out what she needed to do with her work the next day, what she hadn't completed and what she was concerned about. Also, she had fears about what her bosses thought of her and was frustrated with the high standard of workload and production that she demanded of herself. What she did with this demand internally was to treat it as a demand from her bosses, not from herself. This left her incredibly anxious and made it difficult to get to any deeper therapeutic work because there were always the current week's problems to be dealt with which overwhelmed our sessions. I later came to realise that this was a very effective defence on Maureen's part against going any deeper when she felt uncomfortable.

✍ I had to be extremely careful in presenting ideas of change or ways of looking at things to Maureen as she was very sensitive to what I said. She related my questions or suggestions to the criticism she had always heard from her mother. She was physically restless all the time and deeply suspicious of men as, in her eyes, they were only after one thing. This, combined with her shame at her mother's disapproval when found in that childish game, led to an over-anxiety to prove her respectability. This would show itself in our sessions when I asked her any questions about her sexual life. Her attitude was one of 'Is this guy trying to get his rocks off?' I felt she treated me sometimes as if I were a dirty old man.

✍ Maureen did not have enough sense of self. She found it difficult to take compliments and stay with any achievements and successes long enough to build such a sense.

✍ Because Maureen had learned to criticise herself inside without really
   realising it, she was, in fact, carrying on internally her mother's criticism
   of her. This had quite a destructive effect on Maureen's well being and
   relationships. Her answer to all this was to lose herself in work in order
   to be good enough. Like a mouse on a treadmill, she made a
   tremendous effort but was going nowhere. All this helped to shape her
   into a tremendously manic, driven, anxious and often confused
   personality.

✍ The three main parts of Maureen's personality: her Driver, her Inner
   Critic and her Perfectionist, were out of proportion in their influence and
   control over her. This allowed no space for the rest of her to get in or
   have any life or expression.

✍ I had to be very strong, earthed and contained when faced with the
   dominance and power of Maureen's personality. Taking her through her
   thinking and being quite firm somehow empowered her and freed her up
   to make better choices when she saw the effect that her distorted
   thinking was having on her life.

Susi

Susi had been working in public relations for two years since graduating. She was in a stable relationship and was considering buying her own property in London when her chosen film resurrected strong memories of an exotic holiday.

For Susi, the film The Beach reconnected her with an important part of herself and with some happy memories of a trip to Asia. Its impact made her long to be a free spirit again.

The scene that was so powerful for her was where the film's characters were swimming on the secluded beach. That moment — the promise of adventure and freedom with no worries or responsibilities — became her absolute goal and made her memories more tangible. She was jolted out of her 'tunnel vision', determined to reconsider her priorities. She came to understand that she had been drawn into a certain lifestyle by peer pressure, where she worked towards what was expected of her.

The film, Susi explained, helped her to realise she was not being true to herself. She had gone on to make many discoveries that had added more meaning to her life, including her ongoing relationship. While she was in love with her boyfriend, she knew that she must satisfy her longing to return to Thailand and also fulfil another dream of visiting Australia. Interestingly, this second desire sprang from another film, Priscilla, Queen of the Desert, where the stunning cinematography stimulated her wish to drive across the country.

Susi told me she had walked through London to work every day 'without ever seeing a thing of beauty'. She came to realise that the overriding factor for her was the importance of beauty in her life. As she began planning her trip Susie said, "I would not have thought it would happen like this. I'm amazed that a film can do this to someone." She decided to take a job teaching in Thailand 'to give something back to the community through a sense of gratitude'.

Nowadays Susie watches films from a different perspective, finding them beneficial in opening up feelings she hasn't previously acknowledged. The session in which we discussed her reaction to The Beach had proved useful. She says, "I have a deeper understanding and realisation of what I am doing and of my need for more meaning to my life."

BETTE

Bette had everything going for her — a good job, boyfriend, nice house, car, holidays and friends. Yet she was an anxious, driven personality battling with depression. A dysfunctional family background had scarred her deeply, leaving her adrift and with low self esteem. Of all the clients I worked with, Bette found the use of films most helpful, especially The Remains of the Day, Shadowlands and The Truman Show. She used them to gain insights into her own emotional catharsis and to identify with patterns of behaviour. She also found them useful in communicating with her husband. In fact, she was very creative and in working with her over a period of four years I learned a lot about the power of movies in therapy.

When I opened the door, I saw a tall, well-built woman with sandy hair. She wore a rather forlorn expression.

"Hello," she said in a quiet voice and smiled.

"Come in," I said, "make yourself comfortable."

Bette looked quite nervous. "I feel depressed and confused and I don't know why. I have a good job, a boyfriend, nice house, car, holidays and friends. I thought all this would make me happy, but I feel depressed and anxious about everything."

It was most unusual. "Could you tell me what you are feeling now?"

"I feel really sad."

"Do you know what that's about?"

I asked her if anything had happened that had affected her within the last year.

"Yes," she said after thinking a while. "A few years ago I went into business with my dad. He became very ill – he has hypermania. But when he came back to work he treated me more like a general dogsbody than a partner, which really hurt me. And he still owes me money."

"Well, it's not surprising you feel sad, and I suspect you feel angry as well."

"Yes I do," replied Bette, her right hand unconsciously becoming a fist. "How could he treat me like this?" She then looked at me. "I'm sorry."

"Sorry for what?"

"Well, sorry for being angry."

"That's exactly what I want you to do, feel your feelings." Bette looked surprised and went quiet.

What struck me when I spoke to her was a ghost-like quality, a blankness that would suddenly come over her. It was as if she wasn't there.

I noticed she was holding her breath – always a sign of repressing real feelings. I told her that I was aware that she was holding her breath and asked if she could just let herself breathe properly. I wasn't sure she heard me as she seemed miles away. She then looked at me and let herself breathe more steadily.

I felt she was uncomfortable. This is not unusual for a first session, but I just noted it. I also noted that Bette was drumming with the fingers of her right hand on the arm of the armchair. I pointed this out and she looked even more uncomfortable.

"Yes, I'm sorry, but I do want to feel better quickly."

"So you are feeling impatient are you?"

"Yes, I suppose I am." Bette blushed, looking at me as though she had done something wrong.

"It's OK to be impatient, as long as we acknowledge it and talk about it. I want you to share everything you feel with me including what's on your mind now and something of your childhood history. I will be giving you a four page history form to fill in at the end. This session is for us to get to know each other, for you to see if you can work with me and are comfortable. Also, it is to see if I think I can work with you. If I feel, when I know more, that you would be better working with someone else, I will tell you."

Bette looked surprised at this and then her face took on the earlier vacant expression. She just said 'yes, yes' with no eye contact. This was to be her demeanour over and over again, in many sessions. I felt she was disassociating from something that was uncomfortable for her.

"Bette," I asked, "what are you feeling at this moment?"

She looked at me blankly. "I don't know." It was as if, at that moment, she had come back into the room. Then she said, "I feel desperate, that's what I feel. It always takes me some time to know what I'm feeling."

She continued, "I need to get to know you first before I can tell you some of the things I am thinking about constantly."

"Yes, it is important that you feel comfortable with me and can trust me, but that takes time. How does your impatient part feel about that?"

She smiled and intuitively I felt she understood that I was neither criticising nor being confrontational. Rather I respected her and was trying to show her that her impatient part needed to be acknowledged within the session.

"Bette, how did you get on with your parents?"

"I didn't get on with my mum. I could never do anything right. I got on with my dad but his illness made that very difficult."

"Can you tell me how?"

"Well, he would have mood swings where he wouldn't sleep for two or three days and he would spend lots of money.

One day I came home and the fridge was full of champagne from top to bottom, just bottles and bottles of champagne, no room for food.

"My mum couldn't deal with his illness at all nor his mood swings. This in turn affected her mood which made it worse for me. She would pick on me – I could never get things right. She would go on and on about education and always seemed to have much more time for my sister."

"And how did that make you feel?"

"Like an outsider."

"So you felt like an outsider with your mum and your sister and you were often put upon to look after your mum a lot and take responsibility in the home?"

"Yes," she said, a mixture of anger and sadness crossing her face. "You see my mum was so frustrated with my dad's illness that I feel she took out her frustrations on me."

To hear her discussing her inner life no-one would have known that Bette was actually a high powered and high achieving career woman. At the age of 30, and with a powerful capacity for analysis, she was heading towards the top in her profession.

I glanced at the clock. There were about five minutes to go. I explained it was always my practice to let clients know five minutes before they were due to leave that the session was drawing to a close. This was to enable them to say anything they wished about how the session had left them feeling as well as to prepare them for their return to the outside world.

Bette smiled weakly. "My thinking is all confused but I'm glad I have come, glad to have started."

As she left I was struggling to identify what it was about Bette – the mood that she seemed to carry with her all the time. Then it came to me: it was a mood of quiet despair.

Emotional abandonment

At our next session Bette arrived looking quite down.

"I filled in your history form."

"Thank you, I will read that fully later. First, could you tell me if you have ever had therapy before?"

Bette described how she had been battling with reactive depression over several years. Psychiatric counselling had not helped and she had stopped taking an anti-depressant prescribed by her doctor because of bad side effects. Eventually, though still depressed, she had found a combination of medication and private therapy that had helped her enormously. She had then been recommended to see me by a previous client of mine.

"Bette, can you tell me more about your childhood, about your mother specifically and how you got on with her?"

She frowned, looked uncomfortable and started to speak in a very measured way. "We didn't get on. I couldn't do anything right no matter how I tried. Whenever I thought I had got it right she would move the goal posts."

"How did that make you feel?"

"Terrible," she said, face flushing. "Terrible," she repeated, in more of a whisper. "I just felt so bad, so lonely." I noticed her hands were slightly shaking and she held her breath most of the time.

"Can you tell me more of how it made you feel?"

"Frustrated, angry."

"What was it your mother wanted you to do?"

Bette thought for a while with a pained expression. "Sometimes I might be too boisterous or ask too many questions and I learnt not to do that. There were other things like having to look after my sister but I always felt..." Bette never finished the sentence. She just went quiet and again the vacant expression returned, as if she were disassociating from inner pain or confrontation. The atmosphere in the room was one of despair and loneliness.

After some time Bette repeated, "I just felt so lonely, so alone."

She went on to tell me more about her relationship with her mother and her sister. Her early life had been shaped by being part of a family triangle, involving Bette, her sister and her mother. The dynamic was one of power where two often would combine against one, leaving one feeling left out.

Usually, Bette felt that she was the one left out. This encouraged her to start thinking that her sister eclipsed her, that there was something wrong with her. In a desperate attempt to be accepted, she would try to please, adapting to what her mother wanted and valued. By consistently doing this she had lost any sense of herself.

Inside I was empathising with what it would be like to keep trying to do the right thing in order to be accepted by your own mother, but constantly getting the message that you were wrong. For example whenever Bette would ask a question she would be treated as if she was being outspoken. Over the years she came to believe that asking questions was dangerous or humiliating.

I reasoned that the unconscious message from her mother was, 'don't be you'. Be what I want you to be when I want you to be and change when I want you to change. Not much chance, I thought, of developing a healthy sense of self in that. In fact, Bette's constant attempts to gain acceptance and her mother's love were fragmenting any chance she had of developing a healthy sense of self, deepening even further her sense of total emotional abandonment.

There was an uncomfortable atmosphere in the room.

"One of my most difficult experiences was around my sister."

"How do you mean?"

"Well, my sister was the baby of the family, very different from me. If she couldn't get something she would have a tantrum until she got her own way."

"Did it work?"

"Yes," said Bette, looking flushed again.

"So how were you different if you asked for something?"

Bette sighed and rolled her eyes up to the ceiling. "Well," she stammered, "well, that's just it. The attitude towards me was that I could cope, that I was older and bigger and my sister was younger and smaller. So no one seemed to hear when I asked. When my mum did hear me she would ignore me or say, 'Don't be silly', or make me feel that I was somehow a burden to her. She would look exasperated."

Inside, I was beginning to become aware of the lack of any power in Bette's tone of voice and was beginning to understand that there seemed to be a kind of resignation that she wouldn't be heard – the result of her experience of not being listened to. In fact, sometimes it was difficult for me not to disregard what Bette was saying because it was voiced so weakly. This would often be followed by the ghost-like look as well.

"So I suppose you gradually gave up asking?"

"Yes." Bette sighed, looked sad and went quiet.

For me, the picture was emerging of a mother, not necessarily deliberately cruel, but needy and with few parenting skills, somehow lacking empathy for Bette's needs.

"Bette, there are a few more minutes until the end of the session. Can you get a sense of how the session leaves you?"

Bette went quiet. Her face seemed oddly blank. After some time she said, "I never realised how angry I was with my sister. It has been a surprise." With that Bette slowly took a tissue and started to put her coat on in a very slow, thoughtful way. The atmosphere in the room was one of slow motion. She gave a weak smile. "Bye Bernie, see you next week."

As she said this, I was left with the feeling inside of utter despair. My sense was that Bette felt second best to her sister.

Feeling second best

There was a very quiet knock on the door. I knew by its timidity that it was Bette. I opened the door and Bette gave a big smile. "Morning, Bernie."

She came into the session room, settling down in the armchair by tucking her legs under her. "I really think these armchairs are comfortable," she remarked, moving her shoulders in a little girl kind of way. It indicated comfort.

Inside I was pleased because Bette seemed to be becoming more at ease with me. Our relationship – probably the most important ingredient for healing in therapy – was developing.

Bette looked out of the window. "After last week's session, I started to think about why I was so angry with my sister and my mother." She paused. I just waited. "It's because they both always made me feel second best."

"Can you tell me how?"

"Well, my sister would get praised for what she did whereas, if I said something that I thought was good, they would both look at each other knowingly and gang up on me."

"Can you explain to me what you mean by gang up on you?"

She thought for a while. "It's difficult. Sometimes there would be knowing looks which were critical of what I was saying. At other times they directly disagreed with what I was saying. They always stuck together so I was always the odd one out."

"That must have made you feel very uncomfortable."

Bette nodded vigorously. "Yes, yes. I have always felt like an outsider."

"So you feel second best and an outsider. Do you have these feelings outside in your life, at work or socially?"

Bette went quiet for a long time, the room felt quite peaceful. "Well, some people at work do treat me that way."

"What is it about them that makes you feel like an outsider? What feelings do you have around them?"

She sat thinking, breathing very shallowly. She moved from being relaxed into an upright, more formal position, her energy very different now. Once again I observed her body language taking on a defensive position.

"There's a certain sternness in the way some people may look at me."

"That look of sternness, does it have any association with anyone in your life?"

Bette thought for a while and then, a slow smile came across her face. "Yes, with my mum."

"Ah! that's interesting, isn't it?" Bette agreed. But she was miles away so I just let her have the space.

"This is so helpful because I have realised now, sitting here, that whenever I see that look I feel second best, nervous."

"Bette, the experience you are describing is very important in your therapy, because it's known as transference." Bette looked very interested and her mind became engaged and curious. "Can you tell me more about that?"

"Transference is when an old emotional tape, concerning either your mother or your father, gets switched on. This emotional tape plays that same old emotion that you felt in response to your parents when you are around anyone who reminds you of them, looks like them or looks at you in a certain way.

"This transference can be deepened by anyone in authority for the rest of your life, teachers, bosses etc. That is the trigger. When the transference is triggered, you don't experience the other person as they are but as your mother or father. All those unhappy or critical feelings come up, thereby affecting all your relationships.

"So our work together is to dispel that old emotion, in this case feeling second best, since that is how your mother made you feel. When you meet someone who reminds you of your mother or your sister, they act as triggers to make you feel second best again.

"You may feel second best most of the time, but around people who remind you of your mother or sister, you will feel it even more keenly."

Bette looked wide eyed at all of this. "Are there any books?"

"Yes. It is helpful for you to understand. But it is more important that you feel and express those feelings in therapy. As you do so you will relate to people more as they are and not as your mother. It is as if you are erasing a tape."

Bette seemed fascinated.

In our sessions what constantly became clear was that Bette had to look after her mum and her sister a great deal while still only a child herself. This resulted in Bette never really having been a child emotionally.

There was no nurturing for Bette when she should have been receiving it, only demands and responsibilities which were way beyond her years. All this had left her an anxious, driven personality, someone who tries so hard to meet others' demands in the unconscious hope that she will finally secure the love and nurturing she so yearns for.

A telling decision

Bette came in excited. "Guess what? My partner has asked me to marry him!"

"Good. How do you feel about that?"

"I am very excited about it – very pleased." But an anxious look suddenly came across her face.

"I noticed how anxious you look. Why is that?"

"I am worried about my mum and my sister. I'm not sure I want them there." Bette had not had much contact with her mother or sister lately.

Bette sat very still deep in thought, her face dark as thunder. Then she said with great conviction, "I am not going to see my mum and sister any more."

In the following sessions what gradually emerged from Bette quite surprised me. Yet because of her history, it was very understandable. When she sometimes felt down and was talking about her preparation for marriage, she would also think and talk about divorce. This I felt was very sad and I reflected it back to Bette. Strangely enough, she did not think this was unusual but saw it as a conditioned reflex when things went wrong in her life.

Over the next period we worked on that and Bette gradually felt better. However, some six months to a year after her marriage, Bette was to tell me about how she felt about her home.

One day, she came in frowning, looking uncomfortable. She sat quietly in the chair and then that odd, ghost-like expression came across her face.

"Bette, what's happening?"

"I don't know. It's my house."

"What is it about your house?"

"I just don't feel comfortable there." She shifted about, drummed her fingers, irritation in her manner.

Once again I asked, "What is it about your home?"

Bette was quiet and then it suddenly flashed. "That's it – when you said 'your home'. It doesn't feel like my home."

"Can you tell me more?"

She went on looking sad and angry, gradually starting to dispel the confusion. "This house was actually the home of my partner's previous wife. It is a lovely house but she chose everything." She paused thoughtfully. "I have always wondered why I felt like this. Most people would love such a home. Is there something wrong with me?"

"I can really understand why you feel the way you do."

Bette looked surprised. "Can you?"

"I think what you are describing is that this was your husband's and his first wife's home, but to you it's a house. It's not your home that you've made, that you've chosen everything for."

Bette nodded furiously. "Exactly."

As she was saying this, a film was beginning to emerge in my mind that I felt would help Bette. I asked if she had seen *Rebecca*. Bette said she hadn't but she would get it.

The essence of the film *Rebecca* is that the second Mrs de

Winter feels eclipsed by Rebecca, her husband's first wife. Rebecca had that aristocratic sense of entitlement. She was beautiful, sophisticated and wilful and used to being spoilt by those around her. The housekeeper Mrs Danvers loved Rebecca and was in awe of her so she hated anyone taking her place.

The second Mrs de Winter's low self esteem distorts her perception of her husband's real feelings for his first wife. I hoped that Bette would identify with that low self esteem and its distorting effect since Bette had grown up feeling second best in relation to her sister.

I explained, "It is a very good film that is very clear about feelings of being second best. I'm referring to the old black and white one with Laurence Olivier and Joan Fontaine. Just see what feelings it stirs in you and we will talk about them in our next session. But as you seem to like movies so much, if you find any other films that touch you please bring them to the session so we can discuss any feelings they bring up."

Rebecca

Bette arrived full of questions. She sat down and immediately began, "I saw the film Rebecca[1] and I could identify with the second Mrs de Winter's sense of being frightened and uncomfortable in the big house, Mandalay."

"Can you tell me more about that?"

Bette thought for a while. "Well, it was the bigness of the house. It just made me feel very uncomfortable." She paused. "That's it. It made me feel very small."

After a long silence I said, "Can you tell me more about this uncomfortableness? Is that how you feel at home?"

"Yes it is. I just don't feel comfortable in my home."

"What is it that makes you feel uncomfortable there?"

Bette was struggling inside to find her answer. She suddenly looked very young. The tone of her voice altered – a little higher now and a little softer, like a little girl whispering. "I just don't like it," she said, "and I want to run away and hide."

It was a very moving moment.

"Do these feelings remind you of anything in your life?"

"Yes, when I was at home. When I used to walk into my house sometimes, my tummy would turn over. I just didn't feel..." Bette stopped mid- sentence and seemed miles away. She remained with this odd, blank look on her face for some time and I felt I had to say something as my sense was she was disassociating.

Here was one of Bette's patterns of being stuck. It was as if she could not dare to think what she wanted. She was always putting other people's feelings first and clamping down on any autonomous thought for herself. She had learned to do that to be loved.

"Bette, you didn't quite get to how it made you feel. I just wondered if you didn't feel safe in your house."

Bette looked stunned and the inner recognition was very powerful for her. " That's it," she said, her voice breaking with a kind of relief. She swallowed two or three times. "I never ever felt safe."

"So, when you watched the film it reminded you of when you were at home, of feeling small and uncomfortable and of not feeling safe."

"That's exactly right." Bette's face was a mixture of sadness and pleasure.

"In your own home now, Bette, what would you need to make you feel comfortable and safe?" A look of real wonderment crossed her face. "I don't feel it's mine. It's like the film. Everywhere I look there are things that my husband's previous wife chose." She seemed ecstatic at this insight.

Bette now looked decisive. "Move. That's it. I need to move and I need to choose my own house, my own furniture – have it the way I want it."

"How would it feel in your new home?"

Bette was thinking. "Comfy, nice, warm."

"How are you realising that, Bette?"

"Well the kind of furniture, the colour of the curtains, a different place entirely that is new. My house. Our home."

Inside I felt very pleased because I knew that Bette now believed she was being seen and heard for the first time in her life. It was a very important moment in her therapy and in our growing relationship." How can we start to make you feel safer? What sort of things make you feel safe?"

Bette thought for a while. "My teddy."

I have two teddy bears in my session room. I told Bette that whenever she feels unsafe here, she could pick up one of the teddy bears. Bette gave me an innocent smile. "I would like to do that."

"Which one would you choose?"

"Oh, that one who looks a bit scruffy – I like him," she said, picking him up.

"Bette, when you feel unsafe, where do you feel that in your body? Is there any sensation?"

"Yes, in my tummy."

"And when you feel safe, where do you feel that?"

She pointed to her breast bone. "In my chest."

"I wonder what it would be like if you brought the teddy to your chest. See how it feels."

Bette did this, smiled softly and looked quite young. It was a lovely moment. She finally said, "A feeling of warmth goes through me."

"So feeling safe is experiencing that warm feeling in your chest?"

"Yes," she smiled.

At this stage in Bette's therapy I was helping her to anchor her experiences in her body and to acknowledge which sensations indicated fear, safety and love. This is important for everyone but especially for people who live very much in their minds and with logic and who have become disconnected from their bodies and emotions. It is the beginning of learning emotional intelligence.

The atmosphere in the room was very comfortable at this moment, with the clock ticking in the background. Bette sat opposite me with her legs tucked up in her favourite position, teddy on her chest, smiling quietly to herself. I just let her stay like that.

"The book I would like to recommend is *Families, and How*

to *Survive Them* by John Cleese and Robin Skinner. It's a good reference book done in a conversational style with cartoons that reinforce much of what we are doing here in a simple way."

Bette had her pen out and was writing down the name of the film and the book with a sense of excitement. My introducing films and books seemed to have surprised her and made her feel less stuck.

"Bette, how are you feeling about all of this?" She looked flushed, blue eyes quite bright now.

"Excited, Bernie. I am starting to get somewhere. I can't wait to get the book."

We both laughed together. Bette looked happy. It was the first time I'd ever seen any sense of happiness in her.

Mrs Danvers

Bette arrived very pleased with the last session and its effects on her decisions about her life and moving.

"How does your husband feel about it?"

"Fine. I think he understands."

Then a frown crossed her face. "I realise that the film brought something else up in me which was disturbing."

"What was that, Bette?" I asked, fascinated.

"Mrs Danvers," she said quite coldly.

"What about Mrs Danvers?"

"She just made me feel really uncomfortable, like I was an outcast."

"Did she make you feel anything else?"

"Yes, not good enough, just like she did with the second Mrs de Winter in the film."

"Do you associate that with anyone in your life?"

Bette thought for a moment, looking even more worried and said, "My mother-in-law makes me feel like that."

"What is it?"

"Well it's the way she looks at me, with a similar look as Mrs Danvers."

"Anyone else you associate that look with?"

Bette thought for a moment, then kind of gasped. "Yes, my mum."

So once again there was the thread of transference right through her by Bette identifying with the second Mrs de Winter and Mrs Danvers and associating it with the stern, critical or exasperated look of her mother-in-law and her mother.

"Can you tell me more about how your mother-in-law makes you feel?"

"Yes, I feel judged, criticised, that I'm not good enough." Then she went quiet for a time. "The film made me wonder if my mother-in-law compares me to my husband's previous wife. It also made me realise how long the relationship had been between my mother-in-law and my husband's previous wife. I haven't known her long, but they had known each other for 15 years."

In the film Bette also identified with the second Mrs de Winters' mouse-like insecurities in comparison to the flamboyant Rebecca.

She said she didn't feel comfortable when her mother-in law visited her.

"But, Bette, as you explained earlier, it's not your home, but the previous wife's choice like in the film. I wonder if, when you get to your new home, you will also feel much more comfortable and confident with your mother-in-law?"

Bette also had a sense of the relationship between her mother-in-law and her husband's previous wife. Knowing that his first wife was quite flamboyant and sexy and believing that the mother-in-law liked her more, made Bette feel she was second best. These visits compounded her feelings of inferiority every time she saw her mother-in-law.

Because her marriage had brought all her past conditioning and negative beliefs to the fore, I felt the film *Rebecca* would be ideal to trigger all the feelings Bette needed to identify. I saw that the inner conflict between her real self and what others wanted her to be had caused the depression that brought her to me.

Next, she got hold of the book *Rebecca* which she found more powerful. Alfred Hitchcock, in directing the film, had looked at the horror whereas the book looked more at women's feelings, she thought.

More movies

Bette made herself comfortable, legs tucked up on the chair seat. The little raising of her shoulders showed, like a little girl, that she was finally at ease. She was saying she had told her husband about something that was happening at work. Then she added very matter of factly something that made me curious. "I didn't tell him all of it."

"Could you tell me why?"

Bette looked surprised. "Well, I don't know really." That answer in turn, surprised me.

"So you don't know what stops you telling him all of it?"

"No," she said "in fact I do it with lots of people."

Inside me an uncomfortable feeling was emerging. I asked, "Do you do this to me?"

"Yes, but not as much."

I sat there amazed that somehow I had never had any inkling about this. Also I was beginning to suspect what it was that had been subtly nagging me the whole time I saw Bette.

"Bette, can you think why, even in your therapy, you hold back and don't disclose all that is on your mind?"

Bette sat there puzzled and went blank for a long while. She then said, "I think I learnt it at home."

"What was the 'it' you learnt?"

Bette's eyes went off to the right. She spoke slowly as if almost thinking aloud. "It was the way my mother either seemed...too burdened to deal with me or the way she and my sister would make fun of me and criticise me."

I noticed there was something in Bette's tone of voice when she said the word burdened. "Bette, do you feel that you are a burden?"

She looked at me very anxiously. "But I try not to be."

I asked again. "Do you feel you are a burden?"

She repeated, "But I try not to be."

"Bette, it's really interesting: when I ask do you think you're a burden, you answer me as if I have said you *are* a burden."

She looked at me confused.

"You are not a burden. But it sounds like you think you are."

Bette said, "But I've always felt I was a burden."

"Well you need to hear that you are not."

As she slowly considered this she started to relax and in disbelief. "Really? I'm not?"

Gently I smiled at her. "No, not at all."

The relief on Bette's face was profound. "This is going to take me a long while to get used to."

Inside I was still reeling that Bette could disguise so effectively this withholding of her deep feelings.

"Do you think Bette, that you are, and have been, a burden to me?"

"Yes."

"This is so significant that you are now telling me this. Because, when you come here it's important for you to be able to say everything that is on your mind and worrying you. It is also important for you to see the effect that some of your experiences with your mum and your sister have had on your behaviour and your development."

"How do you mean?"

"Well what seems to be emerging is that when you went to your mum with something, a need you had, you somehow got the message that you were a burden or that you were silly and your mum and your sister would gang up on you. If that kept happening to you when you were very young, it's not difficult to see how you could start to feel by their reactions that you were a burden and also that something was wrong with you. You have carried that denial of your needs, and the belief that something is wrong with you, ever since."

Bette looked stunned. I just gave her the space to slowly process these insights and observations.

I looked at the time, realising we didn't have long to go. Bette said, "I'm amazed how these things that happened to me so long ago, Bernie, have had such an effect on my whole life. I would not have believed it possible, but I know – and it's coming to me piece by piece – that it's true."

The Remains of the Day

Over time Bette began to find films helpful in a way that nothing else had been.

She came today very thoughtful and once again sat down and tucked her legs up comfortably and said, "Bernie, something really important has happened."

She said she had been to see a film called The Remains of the Day. It had so moved her, she was frightened.

"How has it frightened you?"

Bette took on the ghost-like look momentarily, then said, "I've glimpsed my possible future in this film." She went on to explain that Mr Stevens, the character Anthony Hopkins plays, is too frightened to express his feelings and his needs, and is scared to reach out although he so wants to. He really loves Miss Kenton, the character played by Emma Thompson. But by the time he gathers enough courage, over a very long period, to speak to her about it, she has left the employment of the house where she is the housekeeper and he is the butler. After many years, Mr Stevens decides to find Miss Kenton and goes to her house by bus, to tell her how he feels.

But when he gets there, he is shocked to find she is married with two children.

At this precise moment in the story, Bette said she was very scared. Inside I was very aware of the importance of this film – of how it had helped her therapeutically. Sometimes it is useful to be scared and, with this in mind, I said to Bette, "This film has given you an emotional experience of your possible future."

"Yes, yes," she said, looking very anxious.

"Well, I think this is very helpful, Bette, because unlike knowing as a concept that it would be good to change, you have this experience which suggests it concretely. Having an experience that frightens you, that represents what could happen if you don't allow change in your life, is very helpful."

Bette was staring at me intently, and shuddered as she twisted a tissue in her hands.

"What was it about this character that you identified so strongly with?"

She thought for a moment, then stuttered, "It was his inability to physically reach out and touch; not being able to express his feelings; being held back from what he needed by his inability to let her know."

"How does that happen in your life, Bette?"

"I find it so difficult to ask for hugs and yet I so need them from the people I love. I know they would give them to me but I just can't ask."

"Well, maybe this is where we could start to focus. Your homework could be to gradually take small steps to ask for hugs."

She nodded enthusiastically, fired by the fear of ending up like Mr Stevens.

I was very pleased at the accuracy of what the film had touched in Bette. I don't know of anything else that could have got there so directly, so deeply and so transformatively as those scenes she had described in *The Remains of the Day*. Up to this point, Bette had not mentioned this inhibition with people although it was very understandable. We had not talked about it. And later I was to learn to my surprise that it had led to a significant pattern of behaviour.

I started to ask Bette who she felt would be the first person she could ask for a hug when she needed one. She smiled and said her husband.

"Is that a problem there? Can you ask for hugs or would that be new?"

"No, I can ask for hugs from my husband but I don't ask for as many as I need."

"So who else could you ask?"

She thought for a little while and mentioned a friend, Mary. "I could ask her."

I tested Bette by saying, "Could you?"

She smiled nervously. "Well, I'll try."

"OK, so this is what we'll work on in the coming weeks. No pressure, just at your own pace in small steps."

"How do you mean?"

"Well, maybe you could get used to touching the person and sometimes put your hand on their shoulder or on their back so that you get used to coming across that barrier."

I was just a little concerned about Bette giving rather than receiving but thought that we could come to that so she could deal with it later.

"Bette, this is your homework, to practice when you are not here. But I caution one very important thing." Bette was looking at me now wide-eyed like a little girl, wondering what I was going to say.

"Just be patient with yourself when you find you can't do it. Don't think of yourself as a failure. You will gradually find the mood, the moment and the confidence to do it and, when you've done it once, it will get easier."

"OK Bernie."

She walked out quite a different woman that day and once again I was amazed at the power of film to be so accurate.

She later told me, "I found this film particularly painful because it reminded me so much of my family and myself. I found it easy to see the consequences of not being brave enough to take these risks. My own fear of rejection restricted the happiness of my own life.

This film made me determined to change this and I started by revealing how I felt little by little. This rapidly gave me such good feelings, not just because I received lots of love back but because I got such a great sense of achievement by managing to say the words I have in the past struggled with."

Shadowlands

Bette came today talking excitedly about another Anthony Hopkins film, Shadowlands. "I must like the characters he plays as they are very helpful to me."

Shadowlands is the story of CS Lewis' love for the American poet, Joy. She is an extrovert while he a brilliant Oxford don, very English and inhibited. Her coaxing and personality gradually draw him out to express himself more both emotionally and physically.

Bette said, "A lot of the things in this film remind me of what I am going through as I adjust to asking for, and getting, my needs met."

"I am so pleased. How is it helpful?"

"Well, it's helpful for me to see how he does it and how his wife supports him. It's just the feel of the film that gives me hope and supports me."

Once again I was very moved and pleased at how a film could be so right at this stage of her therapy, so accurately mirroring what Bette needed. I thought this must be the same for many thousands of people. They might take different things from the film than Bette – but the power would be the same.

Things happen to people as they change in therapy. The old strategies adapted to life, the world and relationships, were linked to the old self. When a person in therapy starts to change and feel better, there is a period when those outloaded strategies can become confusing and frightening because the client has yet to learn new ones for their new, healthier, adjusted self.

For Bette it was no different. She had to let go of those old strategies and would look quite frightened and lost sometimes saying, "I don't know how to do this now. The old ways don't work and I haven't found a new way yet."

"Don't worry," I would say, "we'll just go slowly and work out new ways and strategies together."

My work as a therapist was to encourage and support Bette to stay steady and help her growth psychologically and emotionally. As she got more confident with this asking, and became used to receiving and having her needs met when she asked, her self-esteem and confidence and inner sense of herself began to change for the better. She was always incredibly surprised how warmly and caringly her husband and friends responded to her when she expressed what she was feeling, when she asked for hugs. This changed her life and her world.

Bette later said of Shadowlands, "Lewis finds it difficult to reveal how he feels about Joy and to change the life he has made for himself as a respected don at Oxford. This too is very relevant to my life. I had to let go of the expectations my family had for me and find my own way to live. I am very happy being a married housewife. Yet this is totally against the feminist upbringing I had. This film helped me to honour my own feelings."

Bette's estrangement from her mother

Bette had long ago decided that contact with her mother was not good for her emotionally or psychologically. It diminished her sense of self and always brought up feelings in her of being second best. The same feelings were evoked in Bette when she was in contact with her sister.

Her father was already estranged from the family and they hadn't seen him for some years. However Bette suddenly decided to send her father a card and was delighted with his response. They continued to build a relationship by correspondence, but at a very cautious pace that Bette felt comfortable with.

By coincidence, Bette's mum suddenly wrote to her out of the blue – their first contact for over four years. Bette's sense of shock when she read the letter out to me was palpable. Over the next few sessions we worked on this as Bette wanted to respond to her mother and let her know what feelings these developments brought up in her.

Bette had another surprise when she received a letter from her sister who had found her on the 'Friends Reunited' website. There was shocking news from the sister that she felt she had been sexually abused by the father (Bette had never heard of this), and that, amazingly, she had gone into therapy.

Bette was pleased in one way and angry in another because from her early years in therapy with me, she had tried unsuccessfully to get her mother and sister into family therapy.

Bette's dream

Bette said she had experienced an incredible dream. She was in a small room with her mother and her sister. Her dad also seemed to be in there, but not much. Her mother had a shotgun which she aimed at Bette and fired. Bette was wounded and fell down, experiencing all the feelings of her mum's depression, bitterness and anger. As she lay there, Bette looked at her sister for help. She just looked back at her with indifference. Bette also had some small sense of her father scurrying about trying to help but he proved powerless and ineffective.

When we talked about the meaning of this dream and the feelings it provoked, it had a very powerful effect on Bette. There was significant growth in her outlook. I just offered her possibilities of meaning, asking her what she felt so that together we could find the inner 'click' of truth in it.

My offering to Bette about her dream – I simply gave it to her to consider – was that the mother firing the shotgun at her and Bette subsequently feeling the anger were in fact the mother's needs and psychological wounds being thrown onto Bette to take responsibility for them. The look of indifference from her sister seemed self-explanatory, that the sister offered no help with Bette's needs. And the father, because he was not well himself, had proved as ineffective in helping Bette as he was in the dream.

Bette felt this was the true meaning. I also offered Bette another point – that having the members of her family in this small room in her dream seemed to represent the crowded responsibility that Bette had taken on for them all. She had been doing this until recently, trying desperately to get the family to go to family therapy to heal their wounds.

The Truman Show

Bette arrived unusually late, looking flushed and anxious.

"I've written another letter to my mum," she began. "I really don't want to see her. I am free from her and her views now." This was my cue.

"When you say you are free from her and her views, do you mean her feminist views?"

"Yes, all that," she replied, looking fierce.

"How would she try to influence you with her feminist views?"

"Oh, she would try to put me off men, marriage and children."

"How would she do that?" I asked. I was wondering if this was feminism or a bitter reaction by her mother to her own experience of marriage.

"She would point out examples in the newspaper about men, all negative ones." She shuddered, saying she was out of that bubble now.

"I cannot tell you how much that film..." She raised her arms and waved her hands in frustration at her inability to fully express what an impact The Truman Show had made on her. This was the third session where she had brought it to me and she was still unravelling the experience.

"The Truman Show was just so helpful. I can't, I can't...find words for all the marvellous helpful feelings it brought up in me."

"Can you say what specifically Truman did that really helped?"

"Yes," said Bette, totally into it, "it was the way he leant on to the set, the way he looked up."

The Truman Show is about the ultimate reality show where we are introduced to Truman Burbank, the Jim Carrey character, and his life. Gradually, we become aware that it is all a television show. However, Truman has no idea that his life is actually *The Truman Show*.

The scene Bette was referring to is where Truman finds a door to go through and realises it's a set. He realises he is surrounded by scenery. This is a shocking revelation to him but also liberating.

The metaphor was very powerful for Bette as it helped her to start to drop her old ways of thinking and free herself from her mother's agenda for her. It helped her to begin to find her own agenda and personality and hope for her life.

"What was Truman feeling, Bette?" I asked softly.

"At last," she cried out, "at last there was something wrong, like for me. Oh, what a relief it was. I realised something was wrong but it was not me." She looked exhilarated and exhausted. I sat there totally riveted, observing all this momentous expression of release from suffering and depression.

"I am free," Bette exclaimed with relief. "I have walked through that door like Truman did and now I can go through any door I like."

I was deeply touched by Bette's liberation. "Yes, you can," I encouraged, "any door you like." Once again I remained in awe at the power of movies to heal.

On Golden Pond

Bette arrived looking tired. She sat down in the chair, then asked if she could lie down. (This is one of the ways I work as it can help bring feelings to the surface.)

"I've been crying a lot lately," she said, looking lost.

I realised there was much I still did not know about Bette and feelings that were often too painful for her to acknowledge.

"I saw On Golden Pond yesterday. There was a part in it that really reminded me of my mum and how she made me feel."

"What part was that?" I enquired, surprised at this film having an effect on Bette.

"It was the relationship between Jane Fonda and Henry Fonda, who was her father in the film – how he criticised her. She (Jane Fonda) said to the Katherine Hepburn character, 'I don't feel he's my friend'.

"But then Katherine Hepburn said something that helped me to see things in a different way. She replied, 'He's just trying to get through his life.' It somehow lifted part of the burden of guilt I have about my relationship with my mum – the feeling that it was all my fault."

I felt so pleased that Bette was resolving this burden she had carried so valiantly for so long. I said, "It's as if that sentence helped you realise that your mum's struggle was not your fault or responsibility."

"It was so confusing. "I still can't comprehend the awfulness." Tears were now rolling down her cheeks.

Bette had never cried in four years. Finally I was getting a truthful and comprehensive glimpse of the emotional climate in which she had grown up.

"What was so awful, Bette?" I asked gently with tears in my own eyes.

"For 18 months my dad and mum lived in separate rooms. They didn't talk." Bette could not properly describe that atmosphere of gloom and doom. She was suddenly overwhelmed by huge sobs, her shoulders heavy, her face flushed. "It filled me with dread. I used to dread going home, the unbearable tension." She took a large gulp of air as she remembered it all. "I couldn't, couldn't breathe."

Inside I felt crushed by the sheer weight of it all. "He also cut off my mum's wages. We were all living in one small bedroom, me, my sister and mum."

"Bette, can you tell me how all this came about? I'm a bit confused."

"My mum told my dad she wanted a divorce. This living in separate rooms and stopping the wages so we had to live on benefit, was his furious reaction to her wanting to leave him. This is where it becomes very confusing and hurtful."

"Could you explain how it was confusing?" She took a deep breath and sighed. She felt that somehow, in the build-up to the divorce and after it, she had become completely abandoned.

To help her untangle this maelstrom of mixed feelings I asked how she had felt abandoned.

"Well, I was 16 and it was as though I was put to one side and only my sister had to be considered."

"How did that affect you, Bette?"

"Well, the way my mum chose to deal with her angry feelings was to show me the solicitor's letters. They were very cold and clinical, more or less saying that my dad had some responsibility towards my mum and sister but not me, as I was 16. As I was reading this, my mum said, 'That's what your father is doing to you'."

In her confusion I felt Bette had taken the legal aspect of her dad's responsibility personally. This, of course, had been compounded by her mother's comments.

Bette started to cry again. "It hurt so much I just didn't know what was going on. So suddenly I had to find a job, finish school and I wasn't sure I had anywhere to live."

I could understand Bette's confusion with so many powerful feelings going on all at once. I asked her if it was like she was being used in her parents' battle.

"Yes," she said, "I felt like in the film *The Go Between*. I had to take my mum's questions and messages to my dad and back to her as they would not speak to each other. I was affected by the consequences but unaware of my part in their agenda. It felt chaotic and I had no sense of control."

Clearly Bette had been deeply traumatised by the solicitor's letter and her mum's words. I was also wondering why the father had penalised his children by withholding the money. I asked that question of Bette. "My dad's attitude when I asked him later was, 'well I'm your dad: if you want anything you can come and ask me for it.' But such was my mum's bitterness that I had to choose whose side I was on. To ask for money from my dad would have been a kind of betrayal. Neither of them was going to give in."

Bette paused for a while, then said, "I have just realised something important. It was from that time on that I felt second best in my family and in my life."

"What prompted that, Bette?" I said. I had an idea what it was. However, I did not want to assume and I wanted Bette to give expression to it, experience the feelings and hear herself say it properly for the first time out loud.

She looked sad, worn out by crying and said, "It comes from my not being considered in the solicitor's letter, only my sister and my mum. That's how it feels — it has always been — I'm second best."

With that Bette put her head in her hands. Her shoulders shook. There was no sound, just a sense of her quietly crying deep inside.

I thought once again how our choices and decisions impact on our children's lives.

During a following session Bette announced that she felt really good. "That was an important session last week. When I went home I was so exhausted I slept for hours."

I said it often happens that, when a person starts to express these old repressed unhappy feelings, it is very tiring because it has taken so much unconscious energy to repress them all these years. Bette had been carrying around this unexpressed pain for the last 20 years.

Bette nodded enthusiastically. "Yes, I somehow feel so much lighter." She thought for a moment, "I feel freer." I was very pleased to see Bette more at ease than I had ever seen her. It had been a long hard road with many difficulties for both of us.

Bette sat there thinking. "The major things that have affected my life have been my dad's mental illness and my parents' divorce."

She said talking about her parents' divorce showed that it had affected her much more than she had ever realised. That whole experience of feeling second best just seemed clearer.

"After reading the solicitor's letter, my mum's comments made me feel as if I just didn't matter and made me judge myself against my sister. And not being small and blonde like my mum and my sister but being tall, bigger and auburn made me wonder how I could ever be like them. But I tried so hard to be like them."

I felt I had to make a point here. "Bette, it seems what happened is that you took on your mum's standards in life and her way to be in the world. But it's as if you also tried to impose your mum's and sister's physical standards of femininity on yourself, and felt you were wrong and bad and second best because you couldn't."

She was, I pointed out, very different from them. They were reserved, small and petite. Bette was a much more extroverted personality, auburn and much bigger physically than they were. How could she possibly be like them? She could only be herself. Bette looked at me. "Yes, I truly realise that now."

"And sometimes you talk to me about your past or about your life as though I know, as though I am there with you, about things I have no idea of."

"You know, Bernie, it's so funny you should say that because I do it with other people as well. Like last week when I told you about the divorce. Had I told you that before?"

"Not at all. It was the fullest description of that whole period and subsequent feelings arising from it that you have ever given me."

Bette looked amazed. "I don't know why I do that, but I know you are right."

I was trying to work out what this was. My thoughts revolved around the idea that when Bette came to me she was fragmented and she would give me pieces of the puzzle as they came to her, but would somehow assume that I knew the rest. Was that assumption part of her denial so that she didn't have to visit places of unbearable feeling? Or was it, I posed to myself, the effect of being invaded by her mother and having no inner boundary and sense of self?

As I contemplated this Bette said to me, "Have I ever really told you about the awful things that happened around my dad's illness?"

"Snippets, but never fully. How old were you when your dad came out of hospital?"

"Four or five. My dad was a manic depressive. I can remember that day distinctly. I can even remember what dress I was wearing. I wanted to cry but stopped myself because, if I'd shown him how pleased I was to see him, I felt that would be disloyal to my mum. She had told us terrible things about his illness and what he'd done and how she'd had an extremely difficult year trying to bring us up on her own while he was in hospital."

At this stage I didn't know the other aspects of her dad's illness. We had reached a very important place but now the session had to end. I suggested it might help her and our work together if she felt like doing a chronology of her life to see what she could remember about what happened at different stages. She said she would like to do that.

An issue of loyalty

Bette was looking very relaxed. There was a sense of the inner anxiety and confusion having been considerably lessened. After being estranged from her father for about four years she had decided to send him a birthday card. Somehow she didn't want to be part of his isolation any longer. Very quickly he had enthusiastically written back. This was very helpful to me as her father, up to that point, had been rather a shadowy figure for me.

Looking so pleased with herself Bette said, "I've had another letter from my dad."

She was trying to check the bundle on her lap. "I've had four or is it five?" I felt great compassion for her dad in his hurried response of letters, sometimes 10 pages at a time. I had a sense of him coming in from the cold and how much it meant to him.

Bette said, "I want to read one out to you. Is it this one? No, it's not that one..." There was a sense of real loving excitement about her as she searched for the right one. "I sent him a father's day card as well." At that moment, she was a little girl, very pleased with herself that, yes, she still had a daddy.

"You know, after our last session I said I was going to write to him telling him how I had always felt second best. Well I did and this is his response." Her dad's response was an intelligent well thought-out analysis and understanding of Bette's position, as he termed it, the plight of the duty child, the first born.

When I heard the contents of the letter, I asked Bette how

she now saw her dad. Did she experience him any differently? Bette looked at me momentarily blank and then said, "Oh yes, so much."

"How?" I asked.

"Well, these previous sessions working on the impact of my mum's bitterness about the divorce, mixed in with her feminism, have helped me to see my dad very differently now."

"Are you saying your saw your dad through your mum's lens, rather than how he was?"

"Yes, yes exactly, and I have been crying about that a lot recently."

"Is that regret at the realisation that you had been seeing him in a distorted way?"

"Yes," she cried gently, "a lot of it could have been so different. Much of what happened wasn't necessary and could have been handled better."

I sighed, thinking to myself, *how true*. This sad, fragmented family had suffered so much because of the impact of mental illness, lack of support and ignorance of good parenting skills.

Bette asked in an almost childlike manner, "How am I going to tell my dad that I saw him all wrong, that I saw him how my mum presented him to me?"

"What would be difficult about that Bette?"

Bette looked shocked. "I couldn't be disloyal to mum," she said in a whisper. It was as if her mother was in the room listening and she had to whisper it.

I felt a wave of Bette's fear go through me. "What about

your loyalty to yourself and your dad?" She looked at me blankly as she often did, "But my mum," she said, "I couldn't let her down."

I decided to continue on this tack. "But you will accept letting yourself and your dad down on this issue of loyalty?"

I could see she was struggling to even entertain a new way of thinking and feeling. It felt like what I was saying to her was sacrilege. Eventually she replied, "It feels so wrong to think of it like that, yet I know what you are saying."

"Bette, it feels to me like your mum has hijacked your loyalty and somehow you've got it that she has to have it all and you and your dad none. Is that fair?"

Bette looked stunned as she grappled with what I was saying. Her mother's influence and the feelings of loyalty she had conditioned in her daughter during the bitter phases of the divorce were still governing Bette's whole attitude. She had never considered loyalty to herself or her father. This was a real shock and a psychological milestone for Bette. As she got ready to leave she was deep in thought.

Frightened of getting it wrong

"Bette," I said, "even with me now, I have the feeling that you are frightened of getting it wrong. It is important to talk about how we feel in our relationship in the here and now."

She looked wide eyed. "Oh yes, I do."

And then Bette said a very interesting thing. "I am frightened of getting things wrong, but today I am so frightened of getting things right."

"Really, why are you frightened of getting things right?"

"I don't know," she said quickly.

"That was too quick an answer, Bette, have a think and take your time."

Bette thought for a while. Finally she said, "I am frightened if I get everything right I will be OK."

"And you are not used to feeling OK?"

"That's it. I'd have nothing to be anxious about so what would I do? Who would I be then?"

"You," I said.

I explained that success in therapy is with people who realise they are unhappy but it is familiar. The successful ones can move into feeling happy which is unfamiliar. The trick is to stay with the unfamiliarity long enough until it becomes familiar.

The following period I worked with Bette focused on correspondence between Bette, her sister and her mother which she read out to me. The circumstances of her sister's future wedding forced to the surface in Bette all the painful feelings that had brought her to me, all the feelings of depression and hurt.

Bette's face was a study in apprehension. She sat there quietly holding her breath, in deep thought. The room had a tense atmosphere and then she said to me, "I've had a letter from my sister. She's getting married."

"How do you feel about that, Bette?"

She relaxed a little, smiled and said, "I'm very pleased for her." Then she stopped. There was a silent 'but' hanging in the air.

"You're very pleased for her but what? It sounds like

there is something you don't like about it."

Bette sighed and said, "I'm always concerned about meeting my sister and my mum. It brings up loads of things again." She then began speaking much more quickly. "She's asked me to go to the fitting of her wedding dress and her hen night."

"What's your concern about that?"

"That my mum will be there. I really want things to go well for my sister and I don't want to spoil any of the celebrations but I can never be sure how I will be with my mum. Especially now. I've changed such a lot.

After a pause she added, "I don't know how or whether I want to see my sister either. Of course I want the best for her…" She thought for a while and then said in a voice that quavered a bit, "But I also want what's best for me now." As she spoke she looked a little rebellious and defiant.

"OK. Well, it is good that you are beginning to help yourself in these situations and you are not just having a knee jerk reaction and doing what others want."

"I don't know what to do."

I suggested that she could talk it through here with me, as there was no rush.

Covent Garden

Bette sat there today red faced, angry, blowing her nose.

"Guess what happened?"

"What?"

"I decided to meet my sister at Covent Garden to talk. It started off alright but then, when we got to talking about mum, I just let fly. I just couldn't help it. My sister got angry with me so now I've had a row with her on top of all this!"

We carried on the rest of this session looking at Bette's options. However, she took no decision at that stage.

Not even for one night or one day

When Bette came in she was flushed and looked furious. Her pace and walk were faster and she sat down decisively. "A lot has happened since I last saw you, Bernie," she said in a tone that was business-like and efficient. She had written to her mother outlining her best intentions for her sister's day, to try and get along. The response made her more furious than she had ever been.

Her mother said in her letter that she had assured Bette's sister that there would not be any problem between herself and Bette at the hen night or wedding. She went on to suggest a possible meeting with Bette beforehand but made no reference to their long estrangement nor asked how Bette was.

Bette almost spat as she said, "I've made a decision. I've realised I could not be with my mum, not for one night or one day, without getting furious with her. So I am not going to the hen night or the wedding. I just don't want to spoil my sister's celebrations so this is the best decision." She paused, adding, "I am just so surprised how angry I am."

I asked if she could tell me exactly what it was that had made her angry. "Once again my mum is telling me what I have to do with no consideration for my feelings. I just have to do it because she says so! We've been estranged for all these years but she doesn't see me for who I am. She treats me as if I am still a child."

Bette's position was that her mother was commanding her, telling her what to do like a good girl. There was no question of how Bette felt after this long estrangement. Everything was just assumed by her mother. This made Bette feel that her mother had learned nothing about who Bette really was.

"I think," I said, "this is the catalyst in your history for unexpressed anger about your mum. It's good to get it out. And in the context of how you feel and your concern to protect your sister's celebrations, it is the wise choice even though it may not appear so to your mum and sister." I continued, "You were surprised that you lost control when you met your sister. Now this letter has compounded your sense of how you could not control yourself around your mum."

It was a new thing for Bette, to put herself first. She next read out a letter she had written to her sister informing her of her decision.

"'I am writing following our meeting last Friday. I am so sorry it ended badly...I can't however, pretend how I feel about mum...I am as shocked as you were about my expressed feelings as I normally carry on and endure. But I'm not that person anymore...I have received a letter from mum which has only inflamed me more. This realisation has helped me to make a very hard decision that I will not be attending your hen night or your wedding. I am so sorry."

She went on to explain how difficult she would find it being with her mother at the wedding and how bad she felt that her father was not being invited. She added that she loved her sister and wanted her to be happy. Perhaps in the future they could all consider family therapy?

I gave Bette some space. Then, after a long silence, I asked, "What has this experience shown you?"

"It has shown me the amount of anxiety and confusion I feel about anything to do with my mum and my sister. I don't have to put myself through it.

She repeated that she was not going to the hen night or to the wedding.

"Good, you've made a decision." I was interested to see whether she would backtrack or not.

I felt that it had taken much courage for her to do this. She had made a 180 degree turn emotionally on much of her previous way of always enduring, forgetting herself, all for the sake of acceptance. Now she had chosen to accept herself and stand up for what was best for herself internally, for the first time in her life.

Staying true to herself

"Bernie, things are really moving fast now," Bette said as she sat down. She read out her latest letter informing her mother of her decision not to attend the wedding.

"'…I feel hurt by our relationship and I realise now I will be damaging myself by trying to put these feelings to one side…and I could not do this anymore, not even for one night or one day. My request for us all to go to family therapy last year was my attempt to try and resolve my feelings and improve our relationship.

...I need to hear how you and my sister feel about me in order for me to build a better relationship with you both. Also, I would need to be able to express how I feel and, to do all this, I would need professional guidance in a therapeutic environment, as would be available in family therapy. I do care about my sister and hope that the celebrations go well and you all enjoy yourselves. And it is precisely because I care about myself now, and my sister, that I am not coming.'"

Inside I realised that Bette was trying desperately to stay true to who she was in a way she had never done and was protecting herself by her decision. Also, however odd it seemed, it was a genuine act of love for her sister that she was trying to protect her day from any unpleasantness. But I wondered if it would be possible for the mother or the sister to see it that way and not be furious with her, as was the pattern when Bette didn't collapse and endure. I communicated this back to Bette.

In fact her sister had written back to say she was very disappointed and angry, adding 'if you felt so bad on the day we met, then I wish you had just postponed'.

"She still doesn't get it," said Bette, eyes wide, waving her hands.

"What doesn't she get, Bette?"

"She doesn't get..." she said angrily, "that it was just as much a surprise to me, my explosion."

Her sister, insisting that she would like their relationship to 'only be about us' left the door open for Bette to change her mind. She ended by suggesting 'we could do therapy to help you after July when I get back from my honeymoon'.

As Bette was telling me this I was struck by her sister's lack of empathy.

Bette had steam coming out of her ears.

"All I wanted was to make a connection with my family by sharing our feelings and thoughts. But when my sister said 'when you work out your problems maybe we can meet', I took that as perpetuating the lack of connection and sharing that I so yearn for; a proper family. Her blindness to my emotional needs and her judgemental attitude have made me furious. This blindness is what I would want us to work with in family therapy."

I agreed. "Their attitude towards you is what I think you would also wish to work with in family therapy." Then I said, "I think what is really difficult here is that the things your sister doesn't want, where she's setting up very strong boundaries, are the very things you do want and feel are necessary to heal the family. That's your exasperation."

"Yes," she said nodding quickly, "that's it."

Following all this communication and its dramatic end, the subsequent sessions dealt with Bette's mixed feelings about standing up for who she was, an experience which was very new to her.

As she developed more confidence and dropped strategies she had used when she was her old, enduring, denying self, she became more open to people's hugs. She found herself able to ask for what she needed when she needed it rather than with any hesitancy and endurance.

This made Bette's life and inner life more comfortable and contented than it had ever been. When Bette bought her dog, that was an enormous help to her too. The relationship she had with her dog, taking it for walks, and with the people she met on her walks, started to change her life completely.

One day, Bette came into the session looking quite serene. "Bernie, I've taken up training to become a nurse." She looked very centred and contented in herself.

"I'm very pleased for you."

Bette was both anxious and excited about the exams she had to do. Yet she dealt with her anxiety in a new way, knowing when to let go of what was once obsessive thinking and going over things in detail.

When Bette started to work on the wards, she brought me a photo of herself in her nurse's uniform. I looked at her beaming out at me from the photo, every inch the nurse.

I felt so proud of her. "What a long way you have come."

"Yes," she said with tears in her eyes, "I have, haven't I? Thank you, Bernie, for everything."

It was about this time, because of the shift rosters and exams, that Bette temporarily had to stop coming to therapy. The plan was that she would come back when she had completed her training and got into her shift pattern, The plan only worked sporadically because of Bette's work commitments. But Bette was finding that she could also cope with not coming which pleased me greatly.

In a subsequent session Bette arrived with news. "I've had a letter from my sister to say she's pregnant."

She then started to read the letter which revealed that her sister was in the same frame of mind as ever. She wanted to see Bette when Bette had solved her problems – wanted to share with her that she was having a child.

Though pleased for her sister that she was pregnant, Bette was predictably angry at the sister seeing her in that way.

Over the coming months I did not see much of Bette but she did come to another session. There was a look of satisfaction on her face; not vengeful, but of finally resting. She had received a letter from her mum saying she hadn't been very well and was concerned about not seeing or hearing from Bette. She was quite willing to go to family therapy if Bette could find someone for them to go to.

I looked at Bette as she finished reading the letter.

"How did you feel about that?" I asked.

"You know what, Bernie, I really can't be bothered anymore. I wanted it at one time but they weren't ready for it. Now my mum is ready for it I can no longer go back and revisit it. I've moved on completely. I know it might sound hard but, if she's not well, I'll do what I can but I won't look after her. I am not going into that role again. I'm free from that forever."

A year later Bette received another letter from her mother who again stressed she wanted to do family therapy, as she had realised she was losing Bette for good. Bette said she didn't want to. The time had passed for her. She had her family, her new job and did not want the upheaval.

As Bette left, I sat there thinking how, by watching *The Remains of the Day*, she had been able to experience an emotional prophecy of the consequences for her own life if she didn't change. That was such a powerful warning metaphor for her. The same was true of *Shadowlands*.

Just as powerful, but from another perspective, Bette walked out of the set, out of the show, out of the manipulation of her family culture, as powerfully as Jim Carrey did in *The Truman Show*.

This was movie therapy at its transformative best. Moments from all the films would stay as part of Bette's personality forever.

FOOTNOTE

1   The circumstances surrounding Daphne du Maurier, author of the book *Rebecca*, are very important to mention here. She was in India when she found out that her husband was having an affair with a beautiful socialite. The book, and the character of the second Mrs de Winter, represent the author's feelings on learning of her husband's infidelity. Writing about the second Mrs de Winter was in fact her therapy. When the film was made she would never watch it.

Case Notes

✍ The lack of nurturing that manifested itself in Bette's early childhood continued to affect her as a woman. She had to think and then double check everything which was very draining and made her depressed because life seemed so hard. She was an anxious, driven woman in her life, in her career, and in her relationships. She would fix things, plan for things going wrong. She would look at every possibility in an unconscious attempt to be accepted, loved, nurtured as an adult in the way that she had so needed as a child. This pattern was an important factor in her depression.

✍ Bette was not asking for hugs as much as she needed them, not saying all that was on her mind, because of a fear that she was a burden. This clearly showed how her mother's limited emotional resources had failed to meet Bette's emotional needs as a child.

✍ When Bette sometimes felt down and was talking about her preparation for marriage, she would also think and talk about divorce. This reflected her low expectations of herself and others and her need to be prepared for rejection.

✍ Bette's earlier experiences with her family that made her feel second best were so vividly brought to the surface by our sessions around the film *Rebecca*. These experiences, combined with her inability to express what she felt and what she needed, had their effect on her moods, predominantly her depression. Her fear of rejection, her sense of responsibility as the only way to be accepted and get love, pointed to the emotional turmoil and confusion that Bette lived daily.

✍ In watching *The Remains of the Day* and *Shadowlands* from a third
    person perspective, Bette was able to have the space to observe
    patterns in the relationship portrayed in the film and note similar
    patterns in her own life. Even more importantly, she was able to have
    an emotional experience that she would never forget, about how her
    life could go and the sadness and loneliness it could bring her if she
    continued with those patterns.

✍ She so identified with the emotional loss and despair of the Anthony
    Hopkins' character at the end of *The Remains of the Day,* that it was of
    great therapeutic benefit to her. She felt she was witnessing her future
    if she did not change. Often we can know conceptually what we should
    do but emotionally we can't do it. One of the strengths of movie therapy
    is that a powerful scene can give us the emotional experience and
    insights we need to change.

✍ Towards end of *The Remains of the Day* session Bette wondered
    fearfully how she could change. She realised she now desperately
    needed to do this but asked herself how she could exchange the
    strategies of a lifetime for new ones that were untested. It was like
    being reborn. How could she protect herself in the world?

✍ Bette's dream had a very powerful effect on her and we worked on it
    together. I thought the shotgun and its size were significant. A shotgun
    leaves a round pattern of many wounds compared with the pattern left
    by a single bullet. These were the wounds Bette needed to heal.

✍ I am very cautious about interpreting a person's dream. What I work for
    with the client is their inner 'click' of meaning. It is so important to

remember that you can give the client, on the face of it, a brilliant analysis of the dream yet it can be nothing to do with the true meaning. It is, after all, the client's dream, the client's unconscious, the client's experience. In this regard, we must have humility as therapists.

✍ When we discussed *The Truman Show* Bette had a gradual realisation of who she really was and who she wasn't. She had to learn what had shaped her and to dispel her negative core beliefs about herself. She needed to change her habit of looking to others for nurture and acceptance and to learn how to nurture her real self. Vitally, she needed to lose her self-inhibition about asking for what she needed.

✍ During the sessions which focused on the correspondence, after a long estrangement, between Bette, her mother and her sister, it was a shock to Bette how powerfully she felt. She accepted that she was out of control at the meeting with her sister and gained many insights into the position of her sister in relation to her. She realised she was furious with her mother and with her sister whose final letter to Bette capped it all. It was an intensely complex period where letters were being sent between sessions and this caused a flurry of emotions and communications.

✍ The core of Bette's suffering was that she deeply yearned for love and for someone to be there, but was terrified that the very love she so yearned for would bring about total abandonment and loneliness. Because, in asking for it, she felt that she would drive people away at the very moment she needed it most, she never fully asked or talked about what she needed. She asked a little, but never enough, so she could never obtain nurture completely or have enough peace. This clearly is what happened to Bette's emotional needs as a child. When she was at her wits' end and despairing she would turn to her mother, who couldn't be there for her. So Bette learned a very deep and harmful lesson: you don't share your pain with anyone or cry, otherwise you will lose what little bit of them you have and you will be totally alone.

 The irony was that Bette had always felt alone because she could not share this part of herself for fear of being left alone. This was how, as a child, Bette worked it out. In therapy Bette began to look at how that child had come up with, and absorbed, this belief; and she went on to confront it with me in our sessions. She learned that I didn't run away, that I encouraged her to express her needs fully. I also encouraged her to do this with her husband so that she could start to receive the deep nurture that she so needed from him, from me and from anyone else in the world she could now open up to – for hugs and for sharing.

CORAL

An internet consultant in her 20s, Coral was off work recovering from an illness when she watched the film Shadowlands.

The film helped her to understand her own emotions and behaviour in relationships. As a result she began to move away from the English 'stiff upper lip' culture. "Since watching the film," she explained, "I've tried to make a point of telling people I'm close to how much they mean to me."

One particular line from the film remained with Coral. "We read to know we're not alone," says the writer C S Lewis, played by Anthony Hopkins. He is scared of rejection by the woman he loves. In his mid 50s, he is afraid of allowing himself to get too close to her, fearing she may die. As Coral was telling me this, she realised that the feelings she was attributing to C S Lewis were, in fact, her own.

The message for Coral was that people aren't always around and we must communicate our feelings when we can. She saw in C S Lewis the person she was at risk of becoming in later life — someone who neglects her own emotions for fear of rejection.

Shadowlands had a gradual impact on Coral, starting a process of understanding and showing possibilities that prompted her to take action earlier. The emotional maturity she gained from her experience of the film resulted in an even more fulfilling and honest relationship with her family. She now has a stronger sense of self and of freedom, no longer holding the old façade in place.

By contrast, a second film, Monty Python's Life of Brian, also helped Coral to recognise that we are all individuals and that being able to stand alone is not a sign of loneliness.

For her an important difference between watching films and reading books is that, as with music, she can share the experience with friends.

As a result of her analysis Coral feels she is now a better manager of her emotions. These are no longer structured in a formulaic way but are more interactive, so she is comfortable in talking through issues. A more long-term impact from her change in values will be when she has children and is able to pass on these values to them.

Tasha

Tasha's early years with a frightening, abusive mother haunted her life. Deep down she was still a timid, emotionally deprived little girl grappling with feelings of vulnerability and powerlessness. Her lack of trust in her relationships, even in her relationship with me, her therapist, inhibited her healing. Working in therapy with the film The Sound of Music, she tapped into feelings of safety she had never known — found hope that she might one day be able to let go of her anger and accept what had happened to her. Discussing Shirley Valentine she also realised that anger could be positive rather than spiteful. The film Hope Floats helped her to have a different relationship with a part of herself she called 'the wimp'. This change in attitude was crucial because her normal attitude to 'the wimp' was cruel and abusive and stood in the way of her recovery. It was only a film that could cut right through to this depth.

The first I knew of Tasha was a timid, faint knock at my door. This hesitant start on Tasha's part was a small indication of the great courage it took for her to come at all. I opened the door to a woman with big brown eyes full of pain.

"Are you Mr Wooder?"

"Yes," I replied. "Tasha is it? Please come in."

Tasha smiled weakly and entered. She projected such a strong aura of doubt that she clearly felt she shouldn't be there. This created a duality of feeling for me. I felt immediately protective of Tasha and her need of 'something' but I also felt that I had to be careful not to overpower her sensitivity.

Tasha had a burdened walk and a sense of constant enduring. She wore functional clothes, a green anorak, strong leather shoes and carried a huge, open, worn leather briefcase which was too full to close. To me it seemed that her whole appearance had been designed to hide her from the world. At the start of our session Tasha could not make eye contact.

"That's a big case," I said gently.

Tasha smiled. "Yes, it's my office."

I noticed her eyes darting round nervously. "Are you OK? You look quite anxious?"

"Yes, yes," Tasha said, while frantically searching for something in her briefcase. "I am so sorry. It's my mobile. I haven't switched it off." She looked at me with wide-eyed terror. "Ah, got it, that's it." Tasha now looked relieved.

The sheer level of anxiety Tasha displayed over this small incident took me aback. It was an invaluable moment of insight that I would remember throughout her therapy. At the time I asked myself why would someone be so anxious over such a small incident? The answer came to me a little later. I was dealing with someone who had experienced how dangerous it was to get it wrong.

Tasha was still standing in the middle of my therapy room and then, to my surprise, without warning, she just sat on the floor. It was such an instinctive, quick reaction to her extreme discomfort and, when I looked, Tasha seemed to be in a world of her own. She had a vacant, forlorn look on her face, like a Dickensian waif.

"Are you comfortable there Tasha?" I asked softly.

Her face was flushed from the bitterly cold wind that was blowing outside. Although she nodded, I had the distinct feeling she didn't feel comfortable anywhere. My own unease and restlessness confirmed this. I shivered inside at the thought of such despair.

"How can I help?"

Tasha struggled to speak, her voice almost a whisper. "I, I have…" she stopped, then continued, "a real problem…" and stopped again. She scratched her arm vigorously "with, with dominant women."

"What happens? Could you explain?"

Tasha looked very frightened now. "I just collapse. I, I can't think." There was a long pause before she said, "I go to jelly and panic."

Her answer brought up in me again the mobile phone incident – the level of anxiety she had experienced. The sense that it was dangerous to make a mistake. Who or what had induced such terror?

"Tasha," I asked gently, "who was the first person you felt like this with?"

Tasha's eyes got bigger. They had that look of panic you see in horses' eyes before they bolt or rear up.

She now lapsed into silence. I waited. She said nothing. After waiting some more I asked, "What's happening Tasha?"

Tasha, who was not making eye contact with me or any contact at all really, said in a timid voice, "I don't know what to say."

"Well," I replied, "just say what comes to you."

I was wondering what it was that was making it so difficult for Tasha to talk, or even to make eye contact with me. Why was she sitting on the floor? I felt confused with this sequence of events.

After coming for a few sessions, clients usually feel freer and sit on the floor occasionally. But Tasha sat on the floor as if she knew her place – as if she had no right to sit in the chair. She was slowly twirling her hair with her finger. Over and over she twirled in a haunted way.

I watched her, waiting for a sign or some response. I noticed her face would involuntarily flinch but other than that there was a complete stillness about her. The stillness was one of disassociation from her inner turmoil.

Suddenly Tasha said, "Sorry…" and started to scratch her

arm. Sometimes this is body language for irritation.

"Do you feel irritated Tash?" I enquired.

"Yes," she said, "I don't know what's wrong with me."

Phew! I felt some relief hearing this whole sentence as the session had seemed to drag on and on, but that was my head talking. My heart had a different response to Tasha. It told me to give her time, have patience and care, and let her find her own pace. I felt compassion at her discomfort and distress and wanted to ease the apparent fear and doubt she felt.

"Tash," I responded gently, "this is all new for you. I think we have to give you time."

Tasha nodded silently and stayed like a vulnerable, chastised child. I wondered what this quality about her really was as she sat there on my floor, leaving the armchair empty – redundant somehow. The mood of the room was dead, like a pale cold blue. I found myself glancing out the window and the sky was the same. No relief there for me. I noted this experience within myself of wanting to get away, but I couldn't escape. Again I wondered if this was how Tasha felt inside and shivered.

Suddenly, to my surprise, Tasha almost blurted out in a 'now or never' fashion, "My mother – she hated me." Then she lapsed back into silence.

Inside I was recovering from the surprise of this disclosure.

"Tell me about her hating you."

Tasha's face flinched and I sensed an inner struggle going on.

"I couldn't do anything right. She would constantly slap

me round the head." Tasha stopped again.

"Why?" I asked gently, encouraging her to say a bit more.

Tasha looked out of the window at the bleak winter. "I don't know why. I never did."

At this point I realised that the end of session was nearing and thought maybe this was enough for Tasha. It had obviously been very difficult for her to say this much for she looked drained with the emotion of it.

"OK Tash, we are coming to the end now. I will just give you a few minutes to see how the session leaves you."

Immediately Tasha rose to her feet and said, "Sorry," as if she was apologising for not having done enough. I hastened to reassure her and said, "Don't worry, it's the first session. You have to feel safe and comfortable and you may not feel that straightaway."

She smiled thinly, leaving my house a heavily burdened and troubled woman.

Tasha – a history

Over the next few sessions Tasha told me her psychiatric history. On one occasion, when she had been sectioned suffering from acute depression, she felt that the therapists and psychiatrists she saw had either not had time for her or were not very helpful. However, there was one experience that had helped her. It occurred when, on meeting Tasha's family, a psychiatrist said, "The problem is not your daughter. The problem is you." The response of Tasha's mother to this had been to walk out of the session, swearing as she went.

Tasha's anxiety was such that she made the decision a few months after the birth of her first child to immediately place herself and her baby daughter on the 'at risk' register.

Tasha feared, due to her history and her background, that she could potentially harm her child by 'deprivation of care' although she did not have any inclination to do this. It was an unusual, preventative step for Tasha to take. But her distrust of herself as a mother was so strong, because of her upbringing and her depression, that she often felt unable to care for herself and so worried about the consequences for her baby. To place a child on the 'at risk' register is a step normally undertaken by social workers once they suspect a child is being abused. This was Tasha's insurance against that happening and an act of love.

Tasha's story unfolds

Once I knew Tasha's psychiatric history, my focus was to discover why she felt the other therapists had failed with her. This would give me a much clearer picture of what could work.

During one session Tasha arrived, gave me a weak, momentary smile and again sat down on the floor. The bulging brief case was placed in my armchair. The forlorn, despairing expression clouded her face once more.

As I looked at her, she seemed small on the floor, like a child. I asked myself how this little person on my floor carried this huge case. Although her briefcase was in my armchair, the chair itself looked sad, unloved, unused, and the same mood fell on the room. Occasionally Tasha's face would flinch. Her eyes were wide open, staring ahead, then they would suddenly start to race from side to side.

I asked, "Are you remembering something, Tash?" She stayed silent.

After a moment she said in a desperate whisper, "I don't know."

"It's OK. Just let things be the way they are. I am here if you feel like talking, but you don't have to."

Tasha scratched her arm. Everything was so quiet that inconsequential noises became louder. The clock ticked softly and I could hear my breathing. The mood was subtly different today, somehow lonely and lost. Tasha was now rocking slightly, knees bent up, and her arms around them which was to be the pattern and mood for many sessions to come. Some of them seemed endless. My head would be scurrying around impatiently with questions, my heart disregarding it completely, just telling me to give her time, give her space.

Tasha continued to rock. "Tash," I gently probed, "in the last session we were talking about your mother and that seemed very difficult for you. Could you say a little, just a little, of how she made you feel?"

Tasha reached for a tissue, her hand shaking and said weakly, "I felt crushed, turned to jelly."

"Do you associate those feelings that you have for your mother with dominant women?"

As she looked at me it was as if her whole being was

crying out, 'Help me... like me... I am so confused'.

"Yes, I do associate those feelings with dominant women," Tasha replied slowly with a look of impatience as if to say that this knowledge was of no use to her. She now looked exasperated and was twirling her hair vigorously.

"Your reaction gives me the impression you are feeling 'So what? It doesn't help'."

Tasha, blushing, gave me a lovely smile. "Yes, you are right." She looked relieved until a sudden cloud of anxiety crossed her face. "But I am not being rude."

Once again I saw that same sudden intense anxiety that was so apparent with the mobile phone incident. She had interrupted her relief. I smiled and reassured her that she was not being rude.

Then a strange thing happened. Tasha stopped making eye contact with me, becoming very quiet and withdrawn. I sat there patiently waiting, giving her space. Still there was nothing, no response, not a word, not a look.

I decided to ask, "What's happening?" She just sat like a statue, cold and withdrawn. This was new, unlike her forlorn despair of previous sessions.

Inside I felt frustrated. Aware of how disconcerted I felt, I focused my attention on my breath to steady myself and assess what had happened.

Tasha looked at me with a cold hard stare and said in a cruel voice, "You don't wash your dirty linen in public." The tone and energy of the way she said it penetrated me like a knife. Timid Tasha had gone – for a moment. I had now glimpsed her mother. Then she changed back to timid Tasha and added, "That's what my mum would say if she knew what I had been telling you."

"It's like you're telling me you are doing something very wrong, being here, and saying these things."

"Yes," said Tasha in a whisper, very timidly as she looked down at the floor. She paused for a moment, then said, "Maybe it's me: maybe I am bad and it all never happened. I don't know, I don't know."

Tasha looked very distressed now, her brown eyes pained. She moved her head from side to side as she was going through this inner struggle.

"Tasha, what do you know?"

"That she hit me almost every day. I never knew when or where it would come, so it made me jumpy. She'd criticise me, tell me I was clumsy. She'd scream at me, pull my hair. Whatever I did was wrong."

As Tasha's story was now unfolding, I was wondering what it must have been like to live emotionally with all that shock and attack on a daily basis. Her face twitched involuntarily. Her eyes had the look of a hunted animal. Then, suddenly, they just glazed over as if she had somehow disassociated from this internal suffering.

She continued in a very matter-of-fact voice, "Maybe it never happened." This ability of Tasha to doubt her own experience was a recurring pattern emerging in our sessions.

"Tasha, how can you possibly say that?"

She gave me a withering glance. She was becoming someone else completely, no longer timid Tasha but now someone with sheer dominance and power. "If it was true, how did nobody notice?" she asked accusingly.

"So your criteria for truth is, if no-one noticed, then it didn't happen?"

Tasha was sitting bolt upright. She leant forward and appeared much bigger, not a trace of hurt in her eyes now but enjoying the capacity to inflict it. She was transformed into a formidable woman whose eyes unflinchingly bore right into me.

I felt crushed, with no energy in any part of my body. It was as if Tasha had absorbed all my energy and the energy in the room. I felt both shocked and fascinated because she was also, in that moment, magnificent. In all this confrontational strength and hardness timid Tasha had gone.

I observed my breathing to help bring me back into the moment and regained a sense of peace.

Acknowledging her power I asked, "Where did all that come from?" Tasha looked at me cruelly and spat out the words, "It comes from bitter experience."

"How could they not notice?" she went on defiantly. "Why could no one see what was going on?"

"Tasha, was there really no-one?"

"NO-ONE," Tasha barked back at me, "not anyone, ever." She looked sulkier now, then suddenly timid Tasha was before me again. "Well, there was one teacher, who I think knew something, but at that time people didn't get involved. I am sorry, I just get so angry." But her look was now one of pleading.

I was amazed at the total change back to timid Tasha and the speed of it.

My sense was that Tasha felt deep apprehension. She couldn't escape quickly enough and was deeply relieved when the session was over. Once she had left, my house lapsed into the same silent mood that had penetrated it when she was there. The ambivalent nature of the session and Tasha's behaviour left me in a mood of puzzlement and frustration.

Gradually, over the next few meetings, Tasha started to feel safer and would say a little more each session, although sometimes it was two steps forward and one step back – eggshells all the way!

Once after these sessions, when Tash was due, I absent-mindedly turned up the central heating even though the room was warm enough. I noted that I had done this because I felt cold and empty inside. This was obviously a sign of my counter-transference to Tasha.

My awareness of this incident helped me to understand something important. I needed to communicate to her silently in this period – to show her that it was OK to go at any pace she liked in an atmosphere of warmth, comfort and continuity. She needed to develop a sense of safety that she had never known.

During our sessions I gained similar insights into the complexity of Tasha's nature. Once she arrived and sat down without making eye contact. Turning her head she suddenly saw my daughter's black cat coming up the garden path.

"Oh, is he yours?"

"Yes," I said. I groaned inside feeling that we were being distracted from therapy. Then I reminded myself that it was fine. It was all information and, as I looked at the pleasure on Tasha's face, I realised that here was a wonderful resource.

"I love cats," said Tasha. "What's his name?"

"Russell," I replied, feeling slightly embarrassed at such a stupid name and concerned because the cat was prone to unpredictable attacks on people. When I let him in he treated me with disdain. The feeling was mutual – I felt like his butler. He walked straight up to Tasha who stroked him many times. I was a little perplexed, but now Tasha was cooing to him.

"You evidently have a way with cats."

"Yes, I love them. I have five."

Five! I exclaimed to myself. I have had enough with one, well this one anyway! I got up to let Russell go through.

"Can't he stay?" pleaded Tasha, lips pouting.

"OK," I said wearily, "we will try." Russell just curled up about five feet from Tasha and went straight to sleep.

I settled down inside, the atmosphere now nicer, softer. Tasha looked thoughtful. Then she said, "I was complimented at work today, in a speech given by one of our managers."

I noticed she said it all in a lifeless way, without any pleasure.

"Tasha, I am curious because you don't look very pleased." My observation was made even more acute by the contrast of pleasure experienced by Tasha with Russell.

Tasha replied world wearily, "No, it was nice, but…" she stopped and went quiet.

I waited a while then, "But what?"

Tasha looked angry now. "I don't trust 'em. I don't trust any of 'em."

"Why don't you trust people giving you compliments?"

"They don't really mean them: they probably want something." She paused then made eye contact with me, fixing me with such a look. "I don't trust anybody anyway."

The message was clear in her look and it said 'I don't trust you Mr Therapist'.

"Do you trust me?"

"No."

"Why don't you trust me?"

Tasha went quiet. My sense was she was finding my question hard to answer. She finally replied, "If I don't trust you, it's easier not to let you in."

"Let me in? How do you mean?"

"We would get closer."

"You mean in our relationship?"

"Yes."

"So, in our relationship, you don't let anything good in either. You choose to interrupt letting me in."

"Yes, I told you," she said testily. "I don't want any disappointment, so I only let the bad in."

"Why do you do that?"

"If I let only bad in," she paused, "I can't be disappointed."

So I am beginning to understand Tasha's general defence strategy in life. This way she feels she avoids the pain of hurt and disappointment. In her relationships she will only allow others to get to a certain level of intimacy and then doesn't allow any further closeness to develop. The cost is that these relationships are never enough to nurture her.

"Tasha, I understand that not being disappointed is extremely important to you. None of us likes disappointment but you seem to fear it so strongly. Why?"

Tasha was very quiet, deeply engrossed in thought. Then she said slowly and timidly, "Because, Bernie, if I were to let myself get close to you, you would get to really know me and not like me. You might not see me any more and the disappointment of losing you would be too great to bear. I just couldn't survive that so I don't let it happen."

With me, her therapist, her defence was even stronger because she so dreaded my rejection. She feared that if I were to get to know the real her, which she saw as being as her mother described her, I wouldn't see her again.

"How do you see yourself? Why wouldn't I like you?"

"Well, it's like my mum said," explained Tasha looking bitter, "I'm spiteful and horrible. Oh yes, and she would tell me that I was revolting, selfish and wimpy. While this was happening she would also pull my hair and hit me, then tell me to sit on the floor. I was never allowed to sit in any chairs."

All of this happened to Tasha on a daily basis. Her only escape was school, the lesser of two evils in her experience.

"Your mum would say and do all that to you?" I was overwhelmed by this litany of cruelty by her mother.

Tasha nodded. "She would also say to me that I was ugly."

Her eyes had a sense of embarrassed shame. I was moved and mused on how to work with Tasha on this. I now understood more deeply what this abuse had done to her self-image, to her sense of herself, her femininity and her sexuality, all covered by the huge green anorak, sensible shoes and dark sensible skirt.

"So you have created a framework that allows only the bad in and not the good as a protection against any disappointment or hurt in the future? Have I got this right?"

"Yes."

"But your dilemma is that the wounded part of you longs for the good. The wounded part you call the wimp is living in this barren prison that you have kept her in for so many years."

Tasha looked back at me angrily. "I hate her."

"Who?"

"The wimp," she answered in a cruel voice.

"Tasha, I am very curious. You tell me that you don't want to be like your mum and yet you treat the sad, wounded part of you in exactly the same way, calling her a wimp and saying that you hate her. Why do you do that if you don't want to be like your mum?"

Tasha looked partly disappointed, partly intrigued. "I see what you mean."

"The way you treat yourself, the attitude you have towards yourself is an extremely important part of your therapy. I've noticed you treat yourself very aggressively."

"How do you mean?" asked Tasha defensively.

"When you keep referring to yourself as a wimp, the harsh tone of voice you use when you say it to yourself."

Tasha went quiet, thought for a while, and then said weakly, "My mother was always calling me a wimp."

She had brought this up before so I now decided to pursue how often this had occurred and under what circumstances.

Gently I asked, "In what context, Tash? When would she call you that?"

"Mostly when I cried."

"Tasha, the part that you cruelly call the wimpy part I am going to refer to from now on as Little Tasha, who needs anything but cruelty."

Tasha stared back at me blankly.

"It's clear it's going to take some time for you to grasp what I am saying and even longer, if ever, for you to start to show compassion towards Little Tasha."

I wanted her to realise that the mute child who sits on my floor, the abused hurt child who so fears getting it wrong, is Little Tasha. I wanted gradually to build compassion in her for Little Tasha instead of her perpetuating the cruel abuse of her mother.

"So, going back to our earlier discussion, because of your fear that all your mum has said about you is true, you don't let any relationship develop? And when you do it is only to a certain point in case you are abandoned. Is that it, Tasha, have I got it right so far?"

Tasha was very interested now and very thoughtful. "Yes," she said, slowly looking quite intrigued.

I went on slowly, "So you only let any relationship develop to a particular level of intimacy as a way of protecting yourself from being hurt, should you be abandoned? Have I got this right? Take your time Tash."

"I suppose so," she said, half present, half-thinking. I knew something was going on inside Tasha.

"But this makes you depressed?"

"Yes," she nodded.

"So are we saying, Tash, that you accept living with a permanent low level depression as the price you are prepared to pay for any possible hurt and disappointment sometime in the future."

Tasha's big eyes were wide open now. She looked a little stunned. I was aware that I was asking Tasha to take in a lot. My justification to myself was that I wanted Tasha to leave the session with a new awareness of how her choices affected her happiness.

This was the inner emotional legacy of Tasha, a woman cut off from her sexuality and attractiveness. Outwardly her defence was the practical green anorak, big briefcase, strong brown shoes and short, practical hairstyle.

Emotional cruelty

Tasha came today. She stared out the window as rain trickled down the pane. Finally she said, "I want to see the film Sybil."

Inside I shudder, then ask myself why. This film, I realise, has some similarities to Tasha's experience of abuse. It is a very harrowing true story about a woman with multiple personality disorder, (Tasha, I must point out, does not have this disorder) who has been terribly abused by her mother. The film follows her attempts, through therapy, to discover the reason why she has developed 16 different personalities – two of them men – with one main personality named Victoria who is the memory of all her 'selves'.

I feared Tasha could re-traumatise herself by watching the film, that it might bring up so many horrible feelings she would be overwhelmed. This would not be helpful or conducive to her therapy. Much better to bring up just enough for her to deal with stage by stage.

I decided to share my thoughts. "I don't think that would be a good idea yet, Tasha. There is no point in re-traumatising yourself."

She looked surprised and a bit disappointed.

"Tasha," I continued, "it is great that you feel the film could help you, but could you take the harrowing experience of it, especially with your history? Would that be compassionate to yourself?

I was riveted, my impatience growing at the long pause, but I realised that it was of paramount importance to give Tash space to process all these memories.

My passion to help her must not be allowed to push me into questioning too soon as this could be experienced by Tash, in her present hurt state, as interrogation in the same way her mum had questioned her. It would be, in fact, the very opposite of her treating herself with gentleness and space, so I wanted her now to regularly experience this gentleness in our relationship. What was to come next had the emotional cruelty of the film Sybil.

"Stop pissing out your eyeballs," Tash blurted out in a coarse, harsh, judgmental tone, her face a mask of cruelty.

"That's what she'd shout."

When Tasha said this I flinched emotionally, as I imagined what it must have been like to be treated in this way on a daily basis for years. A sense of being emotionally raped came to mind. But, the most potent part of this outburst was the destructive energy of her words and the grimace on her face as Tasha told me of this experience. In that moment I glimpsed her mother and understood why Tasha had such a fear of being anything like her.

'Stop pissing out your eyeballs.' That sentence went around inside my head over and over again. I felt revulsion for the ugliness of that sentence. I felt corrupted by it. There are some things you hear in life that you never forget.

The power of TV adverts

After the previous emotionally draining session, Tash arrived at the next one appearing much more vulnerable. I felt that, after the hurt she had experienced in our previous session by revisiting the pain of her mother's cruel insults, Little Tasha had been brought to the fore. I felt that she needed all the care, softness and warmth that Little Tasha could take.

"OK, let's just talk."

Tasha made herself comfortable, tucked her legs up onto the seat of the armchair and gave me a weak smile. "Oh, I am pleased to be here today."

"It's good to see you."

She accepted that this time. Some days any comment like that could be met with a look of incredulity and disbelief.

Tasha was looking quite upset.

"What is it?"

"Oh, it's those National Society for the Prevention of Cruelty to Children television adverts. They make me shake. They bring it all back."

Inside I felt a conflict. On the one hand, I had known positive TV adverts to be a very powerful catalyst in helping people in therapy. Indeed, in Tasha's case I felt it actually aided our work together. On the other hand, I reasoned it must be very traumatic for people with a history like Tasha's who were not in therapy and not being helped to deal with their emotional reaction to the strong scenes of neglect and abuse.

"Can you tell me what you think about as you say that it brings it all back?"

"Well, for instance, one of the things that came to me when I was filling in your history form was the question asking what I knew about my birth. When I asked her, my mother would not talk about it. She cannot remember the time of the day I was born. She got very angry and just said it was a normal delivery."

Tasha paused at this point and her eyes looked hurt and haunted. Her voice changed a little. "My mother said that there was another baby, who was born at the same time, to an Italian lady. She said I was so horrible I could not possibly be her daughter and she had always felt there had been a mix up."

I asked myself how much more of this could there be.

"Those ads also bring back the smell."

"What smell?".

"Me," she replied, "I smell."

"What made you think you smell?"

"Because from the age of three I always smelled because I was unwashed. I have a vivid memory of being a bit older and of my knickers not having been washed for a week."

"Tasha," I asked wearily, "was there nothing nice in your childhood, nothing at all?"

She thought for a while. "Well, I remember when I was little going over to my friend's house. I came in through the French windows from the garden and my friend was asleep. I observed the beautiful way her mother woke her up. It was so loving."

Tasha looked so forlorn as she said this, those huge brown eyes lost. "I was so embarrassed watching it, I had to turn away. It was too much – I had never known such care."

I was horrified at such emotional deprivation. "Will you ever let anything good in at all, now, at this time in your life?"

"I can sometimes, if I've told myself often enough." Tasha's reply surprised me as, again, I was to discover another variation of Tasha's confusion. It was paradoxical, fascinating and complex.

"So you have to do a kind of penance whereby, when you've punished yourself enough, you can then let some good in?"

"Yes."

I found it fascinating that Tasha, who is Jewish, was using the Catholic concept of penance. "How does that help?" I asked.

"Oh, it stops me getting big-headed."

I thought I would go further in this enquiry and asked

her what her concern was about being big-headed. "Well, then I would be like my mum. She's never wrong."

I was a bit confused so I asked Tasha to tell me her definition of confidence and big-headedness.

Tasha looked stunned. My sense was that there was deep confusion around this matter in her thinking. She said after a long pause, "I don't know, I'm confused." So I decided to give her a definition of confidence and big-headedness.

"Usually, Tasha, people who are big-headed don't have real confidence. Some may, but mostly confidence comes in a quiet, assured, centered way from a person. They don't generally have to make a big display."

"This is suggesting to me that you sabotage your own sense of confidence through fear of being like your mum. It seems that your low self-esteem is actually a strategy for you not to become confident, which you equate with your mum's big-headedness."

She gave me an old fashioned look as if to say 'Are you sure?'

"Tash, maybe it would be helpful for you to give me an example from your work in how this thinking affects you?"

Tasha perked up at this point. "Well, I would like to go for an assistant manager position, but if I did I'd be terrified of getting something wrong."

"So the frightened child in you comes up at the thought of you getting something wrong?"

Tasha looked at me thoughtfully. "Yes, I suppose it does."

"So your dilemma is that you want to be confident but because you equate confidence with big-headedness you fear being big-headed like your mum. This in turn conflicts with your wanting to have confidence so that you can deal with anything you got wrong. Because you are so frightened of being like your mother you maintain, you impose, your strategy of low self-esteem. Is that it?"

Again I was aware of giving Tasha a lot to take in but these were complicated thought processes that Tasha needed to be aware of to release her from her suffering.

"Take your time," I said, "I realise I have given you a lot to think about in one go. If there is anything you are not sure of, please question me thoroughly until you are."

Tasha looked very thoughtful and said slowly, "I've never put those two together before like that." After some time she continued, "Well, what I worry about is that if I had to tell someone off I would then be like my mother."

"So how does that fit with the part of you that wants advancement with your career and the extra kudos and pay that goes with it?"

"That's it. That's what makes me so frustrated. It's like a trap."

"Well, it's only like a trap if you equate confidence with big-headedness. If you can start to get an understanding of real confidence, this, I think, will change your attitude and your fear of being like your mother."

Bette Davis

Tasha was late. She arrived hurried and apologetic. "Sorry, road works in Elstree."

"Don't worry, Tash, come in, let go of the hurrying."

Tasha's face was wet from the rain. She looked cold. I just wanted to look after her. She sat down in the armchair and snuggled up in a foetal position.

"I went to see my mum this weekend." The familiar look of desolation crossed her face, like a slow, grey cloud. She seemed about seven years old.

"How was it?"

"Oh, same as usual." Tasha adopted her mother's hectoring tone. "Where have you been? Whatever are you wearing?"

Softly I asked, "Tash, is there anytime that she doesn't treat you that way?"

"No, never."

I was trying to imagine what her mum looked like. Tasha said, "She is so cruel. We tried to show her some holiday photos and you know what she did?"

"No, tell me."

"When I spread them out on the table she swept them all to one side and said, 'I don't want to see them'. She then stood up, farted and walked away – that's my mother." Tasha emphasised the word my. She looked furious.

It's strange how some aspects of cruelty have a bizarre, comic element. I sighed audibly and wondered what must have happened to her mother to make her treat her daughter this way.

Then, right out of the blue, Tasha said, "You know, my mother looks just like that actress, Bette Davis, with those cruel, thin lips."

Tasha's face twitched. She went on, "Whenever she came

on the screen I would start to shake."

I was amazed how the unconscious works. Earlier I had been wondering what Tasha's mother looked like and here, 10 minutes later, she was giving me the best possible example, and providing me with more insight into how people project onto movie stars so powerfully.

"Tasha, you tell me how Bette Davis makes you shake and that your mum is volatile and unpredictable. I wonder if you have ever felt safe?"

Tasha looked blank. "Safe? I don't know what you're talking about." It was as if I was speaking in another language – she'd had no reference for safety in her life. What she had was a volatile mother who would slap her round the head and face, then scream at her, "Why are you pissing out of your eyeballs?"

"Where was your father? Didn't he protect you?"

Tasha's lip curled with derision. "He was a wimp and was hardly ever there."

"Why do you call him a wimp?"

"Mum always called him a wimp."

"Why?"

"He would often cry. He was frightened of her." Inside I thought rather comically *so would I be, I think!*

The rain was now pounding the patio door and huge clouds moving through the sky made the room prematurely dark. I felt the room was full of Tasha's mother screaming, her father crying, Tasha cringing. What a life, I thought angrily, protective of her. Tasha at this point was fidgeting very agitatedly.

I realised I had hardly mentioned Tasha's father during our sessions so far and neither had Tasha. "Tasha, can you tell me more about your dad. I don't know much about him."

A look of contempt swept across her face. "There's not much to tell. He wasn't around much and when he was he had a nervous breakdown. Mind you, my mother was enough to give anyone a nervous breakdown!"

As Tasha said this, she laughed and seemed lifted. It brought a lighter note to our often intense and heavy sessions.

The right kind of anger

I heard Tasha's faint knock. I could not see her through the frosted glass paneling of my door. Where was she? I looked out and she was just to my left, out of sight, a long way from the door.

"Tash," I called softly.

"Oh, hello Bernie." She crunched through the snow slowly to the door. She wiped the snow off her shoes on the mat. As she was doing this, she said, "Sorry."

"Come in and take a seat, get comfortable. Are you warm enough?" I went to turn up the central heating. Tasha looked pleased and said, "No, it's just right."

Tasha looked at me sheepishly then with some humour she said, "Here we are again."

"What's the feeling behind that?"

She groaned. "Oh, I don't know, Bernie. Will I ever get any confidence?"

"Will you ever give yourself permission to be confident?" I asked in a gentle but firm way.

"What do you mean?" Tasha looked hurt. We were entering eggshell territory. One misunderstood word from me and she would close down completely for the rest of the session.

"What I mean, Tasha, is that when you tell me about your mother and you get angry, you have no problem with your confidence then."

But Tasha interrupted in a weary tone, "I don't want to be like my mother."

"And that kind of thinking is exactly the place we need to start," I said swiftly.

"What kind of thinking?"

"The kind of thinking that associates any anger with being like your mum. Many people get angry but not cruelly and hurtfully like her." Tasha looked confused.

"Tash, it's very understandable that you have a conditioned reflex to feel anger with your history, but now we can start to work together on changing your attitude towards your anger." As I said this, the room somehow felt spacious and lighter.

Tasha thought for a while. The clock ticked quietly. Then she said, "I will try, Bernie, but it's all I've ever known."

"I know, Tash, I know. Just look at it this way. Do you see people at work or socially who get angry who you think are not like your mum?"

Tasha's interest was now sharpened. "Well, yes," she said slowly, "but my anger is not like theirs."

"How is yours different?"

"It's like my mum's." Tasha was looking ashamed and increasingly timid.

I thought I would put the question another way. "OK, Tash, how is your mother's anger different?" Tasha sat and thought for a long time.

"She attacks – tries to hurt you."

"How is that different from people at work?"

Tasha thought again. "They make their point but don't attack people personally."

"Great, so you're already learning very important distinctions between anger and self-assertion."

Tasha looked thoughtful. "I've never understood that."

"What? Self assertion?"

"Yes," replied Tash sadly.

Tasha and I continued during this session to work with this cognitive but very important emotional re-education because, while a person can understand something conceptually, that is not enough to change their emotional feelings. As Tasha's inner and external awareness increased, the potential for change was enhanced.

So how could I give Tasha an emotional experience that she could connect to as an anchor in herself for healthy anger or self assertion?

"Tash, I think it's important for you to start to value your own anger as a bridge towards self-assertion and confidence."

Tasha looked frightened, listened timidly and seemed hesitant.

"How are you feeling now, at this moment? What are

you aware of?"

"I feel frightened, shaky," she replied in a small voice.

Then I realised I hadn't enough time. The session was drawing to a close.

Tasha looked at me. "It's time. I must hurry. I have to see a client." The session ended and I was left pondering the way forward.

I felt frustrated and disabled. How could I show Tash how this conditioned reflex to anger disabled her? Her revulsion regresses her to the state of a child once again, facing her mum in paralysed terror. But this unconscious mechanism switches so fast that Tasha is completely unaware of how it happens. For her it was a most effective defence against becoming – as she saw it – like her mother. But, to further complicate matters, there was another extremely important component. Her memory of her mother's frightening attacks on her.

So how could we comfort the terrified little girl in her – reassure her, help her feel safe from her mother's past attacks in the present?

Uncomfortable truths

Tasha arrived and, as she was taking her coat off, she looked out of my patio doors. Her manner, which had been tentative, now changed.

"I see you still haven't cut the grass." This was delivered with such a withering coldness I felt like I had been cut in two. She had a smile on her face as if to show she was only teasing. But the icy contempt for me was the deepest communicated message.

"You seem angry with me?"

She acted surprised. "No, I am not angry." She said this in a way that made me feel humiliated. There was a slight smile of pleasure on her face as she saw me squirm.

I could not bear the discomfort and attempted to laugh it off. This didn't work and I was feeling that I had to escape the discomfort, get some relief.

Tasha decided to spare me, "Bill has not done our hedges. Its always 'I'll do it tomorrow'. That's him, Mr Mañana man."

I laughed with relief, glad that Bill, her partner, was getting it and not me. Now that I had regained some equilibrium, I realised my counter transference, that is all the uncomfortable feelings I had just experienced – the humiliation, the squirming, the overwhelming discomfort, my cowardice in laughing it off – were all the feelings that Tasha had been brought up with.

"Tash, do you nag Bill and me like your mother nagged you?"

Tasha looked blank then became timid Tasha. She looked frightened, upset. "I am sorry, I don't mean to … I don't want to be anything like her. I feel physically sick." Tasha went white. She started gulping, swallowing. There was a possibility she would be sick. I looked for my waste paper bin out the corner of my eye in case I needed it. Tasha started to make retching noises.

"Here, Tash, don't worry, be sick in there." I placed the

bin at her feet. Tasha was not sick. Gradually she settled down, squirming with shame and humiliation.

The atmosphere in the room was strange, toxic. Tasha was drying her eyes, blowing her nose with the tissues. I felt exhausted.

"How are you Tasha?" I asked softly.

She smiled back weakly. "Dizzy. I just cannot stand the thought of being like her." She shuddered.

I knew I had to be honest with her and not collude with her denial, but that I must do it with compassion in a way that did not devastate her.

"Tash," I suddenly heard myself saying, "sometimes you are like your mother – but only sometimes, only sometimes, not all the time. You cannot not be influenced by your mum at all. It wouldn't be possible. You are very, very different from your mum. You have had the courage to come to therapy, to work on all this. You have chosen and shown real commitment. Your mum couldn't and wouldn't do that and that is only one of the fundamental differences between you."

Tasha took my comments well and smiled at me. "I must remember that."

"Don't worry, I'll say it regularly so you don't lose it."

Tasha looked at my clock and started to get ready to leave. "Bye, Bernie," she said, adding with a searching look, "Do you still like me?"

"Of course, I do, more so."

"Why?" she asked, looking reassured but puzzled.

"Because of your courage, Tash, your courage. I know

this is so difficult for you." She looked pleased.

"Thanks Bernie," she said, and I waved goodbye to her.

Shirley Valentine and the Sound of Music

Tasha came today dressed differently. She was wearing a white blouse and a blue floral patterned skirt and, seeing her in those clothes, I became much more aware of her as a woman. She sat down, stared out of the window and was thoughtful for a long time.

"I am finding it really difficult to understand what you are saying about anger, Bernie."

"What's difficult?"

"Well, I just can't see anger in any other way than how my mum is."

"Tash, have you seen the film *Shirley Valentine*?"

"Yes," she said enthusiastically, looking quite surprised.

"Well, do you remember the scene where Shirley is in the kitchen, her husband has just thrown the dinner, and this is the straw that breaks the camel's back? She decides to go on holiday to Greece. But instead of just thinking about it as in the past, she is galvanised into action by her anger – it is the thing that helps her. This is an example of positive anger – how it can motivate you to act. So that is the kind of anger I am talking about as opposed to the vindictive anger which I think you see from your mum and which you fear from yourself."

"I'll have to think about that."

"OK."

Realising that she had responded very quickly to the mention of that film I wondered if there were any others she has really liked that may have helped her.

"Tash, talking about films, is there any film that you find has helped you?"

A big smile came across Tasha's face as if to say, I like this. It's not like therapy.

"I love *The Sound of Music*."

Inside I groan. I can't stand *The Sound of Music*. However, what followed was truly moving.

"Tell me, what is it you really like about the film? Is there anything that helps you?"

Tasha got comfortable. "I never tire of seeing this film. I think it represents my ideal family childhood. The children look out for each other and when Maria (the governess) arrives she teaches them how to love and have fun." Tasha paused.

I was very excited that Tasha was gaining so much from this film. The fact that she was so articulate and had evidently thought about it a great deal was even more impressive.

"Is there anything else, Tash?"

"Yes, Maria. She is firm and friendly and gives love without emotional blackmail. And the children are sad about the distant relationship they have with their father, but not depressed. In fact, they seem to have an inner strength and they believe that they are worth something. There does not seem to be any destructiveness in this family." Tasha said this with a look of regret and hurt in her eyes.

She sighed and moved about restlessly. I was sitting there in rapt attention. "Each time I watched this film, it helped me to escape into a world of happiness and love I so longed for. I knew the words to all the songs and, if I went for a long walk on my own, I would sing them to cheer myself up and give myself the energy to keep going and escape from hurting."

What Tasha had just told me was deeply moving and impressive. She had found a healthy inner resource and she had done it all on her own, which was terrific. As Tasha sat there quietly I asked gently, "Is there anything else, Tash, that comes to mind about the film?" She thought for a long time. Then I saw her nod quietly to herself.

Tasha stretched both arms out and looked quite relaxed. "I admired the way the children stood together against the bitchy countess with the thin plucked eyebrows who reminded me of my own mother." Tasha now looked frightened. "I felt the paralysis and fear when the Nazis came and admired the way Maria and the Captain did not appear to be bullied by them. Although they must have been afraid, they remained strong for the children and helped them to feel safe." Tasha stopped there, looked sad and seemed to float away. Then she said in a heartfelt way, almost unconsciously, "I would have loved to have felt safe and held."

Once again I found this incredibly sad and moving but I thought how helpful this could be in Tasha's therapy. "When did you last watch it, Tash?"

"Ten days ago, I think." She was thoughtful again. "I suppose at this stage in my therapy when I see this film, it helps me to accept that I truly had a rotten abusive childhood, with no love."

Then she said something with a kind of maturity and wisdom that I hadn't expected. "Some parents do have both warmth and love for each other and their children. They just weren't my parents."

In Tasha's final comment about *The Sound of Music* she said, "The end of the Edelweiss scene, when the children run to their father and forgive him, gives me hope. Now I think that perhaps one day I will be able to let go of my anger and accept what happened to me."

I realised the session was drawing to a close. I was lost in the whole emotional mood of what Tasha had told me and I just needed time to be quiet and see what it brought up for me. I knew from experience that this was a breakthrough in Tasha's therapy.

Tasha got up slowly and gave me a look – real eye contact that had genuine affection in it for me. I smiled back, still a little choked inside. "Bye, Tash." I was surprised as I became aware of the softness of my tone. She must have clearly seen how moved I was.

Over the following week I gave much thought to establishing a clearer picture of what *The Sound of Music* had given Tasha and how. My reasoning was that to go more deeply into it would be beneficial to her. She did let good in. A more complete picture was now emerging of the unconscious choices she was making in order to manage her nurture and abusive treatment of herself.

She seemed to think that she only let bad in. If she punished herself, however, she would allow some good in and with film there was a veritable feast of good. So how did she make these choices? Was it easier for her with a film, one that wouldn't hurt her, and over which she had control? I resolved to ask her what else helped her.

Safety replaces terror

Tasha arrived and to my surprise said, "After our session last week Bernie, I decided to watch *The Sound of Music* again." Inside and outside I had a great big smile. Sometimes the therapist gets a gift of what to work with in a session – and here it was.

"Tasha, I wonder if we could look at what *The Sound of Music* actually gives you." Tasha thought for a while as she placed her legs over the arm of the chair, revealing a considerable part of her leg and thigh, and sat sideward looking out of the patio window, as she often does. I noted this display of her legs to me which was an unconscious new feature of our sessions.

Tasha then turned to me and she said, "Well, I can decide when I want to see it. I can watch it when I need to."

"So it gives you control?"

"Yes." Tasha looked quite pleased with herself.

"What else do you think it gives you?"

Tasha paused for a while and then said very clearly, "Reliability. It's simply always there waiting to be seen. It won't let me down."

The session proved most revealing. I could have just taken a cursory interest in the fact that Tasha liked *The Sound of Music* but, as her answers to my questions showed, the film was a much more comprehensive resource than had been immediately apparent.

"Just carry on thinking about scenes from the film and anything else that you may have drawn from it."

Tasha smiled, bent her left leg up so there was only one leg straight and the left one in front of me, exposing even more of her buttocks.

With this display of Tasha's legs, I was caught between which direction to take. On the one hand I wanted to get to what was helpful to Tasha about the film. On the other hand this was a powerful unconscious display of something that couldn't be ignored.

"Tasha, are you aware of how much of your leg you are displaying to me?"

Tasha turned her head and looked at me, her face full of embarrassment. "What do you mean?" she asked, quickly pulling down her skirt.

"Simply what I just said – that you are showing a lot of leg to me and are you aware of that?"

Tasha looked at me sulkily, "Well, I'm wearing a long skirt." I did not reply to this. She went quiet.

"My role here is to mirror back what happens in our relationship. It's fine if you want to show me your legs – they are very nice – but we both need to be aware of it and that's why I am mentioning it."

"Men!" Tasha said.

"Women!" I jokingly replied. A glimpse of a smile went across Tasha's face and she returned to the film.

What Tasha said next was very interesting, taking into

account the sexual nature of what had just happened. "Safety, the film gives me safety. I know it's there and it works. It helps me feel safe when I am frightened."

My mind was thrown back to previous sessions where she had no idea what safety was. Here, discussing the film, and two years into our relationship, she was talking about experiencing safety. What a wonderful thing to happen. Safety was gradually replacing terror.

"Tasha, you say that with such confidence. I am really getting a deep understanding of how helpful this film is to you."

"Well, to be honest, as I am talking about it to you, so am I."

"Would you say that the film also gives you confidence? And your ability to help yourself when you are feeling vulnerable?"

"Oh yes, it does."

Time is moving on and I note that Tasha is once again showing a considerable part of her leg.

"Tasha, it's a few minutes before ending. How has the session left you?"

"Well, a bit mixed really, pleased about the film but uncomfortable about what you said." Tasha stopped and froze. Her hand shot down to her skirt, as she realised once again, she was showing her leg to me. She looked rather embarrassed and angry as she got up and left. And she gave me a kind of cold throwaway line as she went out the door. "I'll wear trousers next week."

"OK." I was feeling rebuked as if somehow it was my

fault. This, once again, was the counter transference of Tasha feeling she had done something wrong by showing her legs to me.

It was becoming clear to me what was happening. When Tasha was showing her leg to me, she was unconsciously tapping into her teenage flirting years that had been undeveloped around her father. This can happen if a young girl, going through puberty, is not appreciated by her father as becoming a beautiful young woman. If she can't flirt with her dad, get round him, charm him, she often has a problem in being confident in her sexuality and femininity and subsequently in her relationships with men. This was Tasha's experience, compounded by the abuse by her mother.

A possible breakthrough

Some months ago, Tasha had emailed me, sobbing while she did it, to say that she had just seen a film called *Hope Floats*. The scene where the father leaves the little girl had left Tasha sobbing uncontrollably in a way she could only remember doing once or twice before in her life.

When she came to see me after sending me the email, it was impossible to work with the pain that the film had brought up in her. I was deeply frustrated because I felt there was something very important and new about the way Tasha had reacted to this film. My intuition was that she was on to something but I felt I had to let it go for the meantime. Maybe one day we would return to it.

A few sessions passed before Tasha once more brought up the subject of *Hope Floats*. She had been scanning the TV channels for a suitable programme when she found the film was on again. She said she had been forced to leave the room during the same scene.

Again I thought how important this was as I had been talking to Tasha about her hatred of Little Tasha, and her inability to feel any compassion still for Little Tasha. I wondered aloud to Tasha whether, maybe for the first time, she was experiencing the true despair and desolation of Little Tasha in her cruel, emotionally barren prison. I felt the film and the scene had touched the depth of Little Tasha's experience of total and complete abandonment by everybody for some 50 years.

Tasha looked at me wide eyed. "But how can I get to love her? I know nothing else, Bernie. You don't seem to understand."

"But you always call her 'dirty, horrible and a wimp', so tell me, specifically, what is dirty, what is horrible and what is wimpish about her?"

Tasha glared back at me, eyes blazing in angry desperation. "I can't tell you. I can't tell you. It's just all I've ever known. It's just with me, Bernie". She was incredibly angry with me.

I said to Tasha firmly, "No, what I would like you to entertain, Tash, is that this is an old, abusive tape of your mother. It would help if you could slow this down and tell me exactly what happened step by step. What would your mum say or do, what would start it, what was the trigger for your mother's abuse of you?"

Tasha thought for a moment. "It was always when I

started to cry and answered her back. She would say, 'I'll knock all that out of you'."

What she was 'knocking out' of Tash was any independent, healthy sense of self and replacing it with a sense of terror so that she could control Tasha's every move, even her thoughts.

The important new thing that emerged in this session was when I asked Tasha about her relationship to the wimpish part of her. It was clear she now blamed that part of her for all the suffering her mother had inflicted upon her any time she saw any of those characteristics emerging. Tasha just wished they weren't there and hated them.

Until this time I had thought only that Tasha was replaying the tape of what her mother had always said about the wimpish part. But this added a new dimension. She had a real reason to hate that part for, whenever she displayed independence, any crying or vulnerability, her mum would hit her and say, "I'll knock that out of you." This in turn made Tasha hate those feelings and the part of her that felt them because the consequences were abuse and terror.

Somehow I had to bring Tasha into the 'now' and by some experience show her that her vulnerability and independence would not bring her abuse or suffering but freedom from emotional pain. We would have to visit this area many times for her to have a healthy therapeutic experience of that time of her life.

"What I am asking you to do now, from this moment on, is to start to think for yourself why this poor child is so revolting. I am also asking you, when the sobs come to you in watching *Hope Floats*, to realise that what you feel is because you've treated little Tasha, who is suffering, so cruelly all these years."

Tasha looked stunned and her face softened. "I feel a little guilty." Inside, I am beside myself. After years and years here is the first glimmer – some healthy guilt in Tasha – as she glimpses her cruelty towards Little Tasha. This is a great day for Tasha that she realises and an even greater day for Little Tash.

My reaction was that I wanted Tasha to see this film and to hold her while she watched it. Once again I felt that this was my counter transference. Actually Tasha wanted me to hold her physically while we watched the film. However this would confuse her right now so we would have to see where the process took us.

As we were about to end the session I asked, "Would you like to watch the film with me and work on that moment and what it brings up in you? You don't have to. It's your choice."

Tasha looked at me frightened, then smiled. "OK. Can you get the film though?"

At that moment I felt like a dad with a little girl who was too young to get the film herself. I said I would and we agreed to start directly with the film next time we met. Tasha left looking anxious and excited at the same time.

Hope Floats

Tasha is due for our session to watch *Hope Floats* together. The particular scene in *Hope Floats* that so moves her is the scene where the father has asked his wife for a divorce. While this conversation is going on, the young daughter aged about eight is watching through the garden door. She can't quite grasp the significance of her daddy leaving so, as he goes to the car, she just puts everything in a bag, walks down past her mum at the front of the house and says, 'I'm going with my daddy'. She calls out to her daddy with confidence, certain that she is going with him until he turns round and says, "No you can't. You have to stay here with mummy, as I have to start a different life now: me and mummy are not happy."

Before he can get into the car, the little girl swiftly opens the back door, throws in her little bag and jumps in. The dad comes round and lifts her out of the car and she starts to scream. It gradually gets louder, "No, no daddy, no, no." As he takes her holdall out of the car, puts it on the road and starts to drive away, her screams get louder and she starts to sob as she pitifully runs after the car. The screaming becomes unbearable.

Her mother, who realises that the little girl has to face this reality, is sitting on the porch observing this. The car disappears out of sight and the little girl physically slumps and sobs, realising her powerlessness to do anything about it. When her mother walks up to her the child jumps into her arms and her mum just hugs and holds her tightly, carrying her back to the house.

This scene, particularly the sound of the screaming, was unbearable for Tasha. It cut right through her defences to that vulnerable part of her she called the wimp.

Feeling powerless

Tasha knocked on the door, came in looking nervous, but smiling at me. I just asked as we sat down, "OK, do you still want to watch it?"

"Yes," she said, snuggling up in the chair.

I got Tash to sit on the settee and I pulled up an armchair beside her, so the arm of the settee and the arm of my armchair were touching.

I had already pre-set the scene and just pressed the video to start. I glanced at Tasha, not wanting to be too intrusive to her reaction to what she was watching. Her eyes became sad and lost but I noticed something odd. Her cheeks, her face – they just seemed lifeless.

The scene does not last very long, but the screams of the little girl, made it seem interminable. We got to the bit where the little girl is picked up by her mother and I switched off the video. I looked at Tasha who was quiet and withdrawn and I said gently to her, "You have just heard the screams of a wimp, someone horrible, revolting."

Tasha responded with a shocked "No," then went silent. After some time she said, "It's different watching it with you. I couldn't feel much at all."

I was disappointed but not entirely surprised.

"I think that because I knew I was coming to do this, I blanked off. I really defended myself."

"OK, but what would you say was the bit that touches you the most in this scene?"

"Well, I could identify with the little girl as she was not a classical beauty. It made me think of my own daughter and wonder if I have been a good mother."

"Well, you've always been there to pick your daughter up and in the film the mother was there to pick up and comfort her daughter during her greatest pain and suffering. But when you went through your experiences there was no-one, absolutely no-one there to pick you up. No-one to hold you, to hold you that way that comes up in me. To hold that little girl in you."

This was a very important moment. I wanted to hold the child in Tasha, clearly communicating that this was nothing to do with sexuality, but the emotional nurture of a deprived, powerless little girl.

Tasha's body twitched and she went quiet. "That's what it is, the powerlessness. That little girl was powerless and that's how I felt from such an early age. I just felt so powerless."

I continued, "What I want you to think about is your powerlessness and how you identify with this little girl. It's the Little Tasha in you that is identifying with her, the part that cannot bear the little girl's screams and sobs. It is the little girl in you, but you continue to call that part of you revolting, wimpish. You are always telling me that you don't want to be like your mother but that is precisely the way you are treating the little girl in you."

Tasha looked across at me, very uncomfortable. "You are asking me, Bernie, to be nice to it? It makes me feel physically sick."

Tasha's hand moved unconsciously to her tummy. "You are asking me, Bernie, to be nice to something that brings up only revulsion in me."

I was considering how to work with this, with what had always appeared to be immovable. Then I had an inspiration.

"OK, Tash, I want you to watch the scene again with the little girl sobbing and I want you to tell the little girl out loud that she is horrible. She makes you feel sick. You feel only revulsion for her."

Tasha was shocked and appalled at my suggestion. "No," she gasped, "no, I couldn't do that." "So why do you keep doing it to yourself?" Tasha looked stunned. It was such a powerful moment.

Tasha was very quiet. She looked confused. I was aware of the struggle that was now going on inside her after my suggestion that she shout at the little girl. She was having to come to terms now with something in spite of herself.

Making her shout the abuse at the little girl she identified with on the screen shocked Tasha into realising how difficult that was but how easy she found it to say it to herself inside. This brought about a different attitude towards the wimpish part of her in a way I don't think anything else could have done.

For the very first time a tear started to trickle down Tasha's cheek. "It's not true that she's horrible."

"No," I said, "it never was."

This was amazing. I had never seen Tasha cry in any session. She cried on her own as she had been used to doing all her life, in her car where no one could see her. For her to share her crying was a major breakthrough in her fear of being vulnerable with me.

Tasha looked at me, looked at my hand on the armchair and moved away slightly. She decided to go on the attack in an area she felt was uncomfortable for me. "I know you want to touch my hand. And that frightens me."

"No, Tash," I replied firmly, "my hand is there for you to take if you wish. It has nothing to do with me wanting to touch your hand, but everything to do with the little girl in you choosing to risk, after all these years, reaching out to someone who is here now."

Tasha's eyes glazed over with tears. She said in a very gentle voice, "Bernie, I fear if I take your hand, I will be vulnerable and then I will feel powerless."

"What is it about feeling powerless and vulnerable with me?"

After another long pause she whispered in a very young voice, "I am frightened to take your hand in case you go." As she said 'go' she did a huge swallow as if she were holding something back. She continued, "But I'm also frightened not to. I'm frightened to miss this chance that you are offering me."

"No rush, Tash, maybe one day you will be able to reach out."

I clearly had to re-direct her to the fact that my hand was there for her to take and that it was in fact an invitation to little abused Tasha to make contact for the first time with anybody. If she gave herself permission to reach out, the spell of powerlessness for little Tash would be broken and she would have taken the first steps towards nurture, connection and autonomy. Would she take that opportunity since *Hope Floats* had so deeply touched that part of her for the first time in her life?

Tasha was openly crying now. She took my hand and, gradually, held it tighter.

After some time of her holding my hand, it was time for the session to end. Tasha said, "Bye Bernie," with much more affection in her voice than ever before. What a breakthrough!!

Tasha today

Tash and I continue to work towards her no longer needing to come to therapy. She is now a successful manager at her organisation and continues to improve in all areas of her life.

For her feelings and her life to be much more comfortable, she has learned a number of very important lessons. She is able to take the emotional charge out of any old feelings that come up again and to manage them much more efficiently. She knows what she needs to do to bring herself back to her centre. When she experiences some unhappy moment in her life or a big shock, she understands that she will temporarily go back to her old way of reacting. But she also knows this reaction will not last and she will come back to her new self quickly. Most importantly, she has learnt how to start to nurture the wimpish part of herself or 'Little Tasha' and continues to get better at practising this.

Case Notes

✍ I have long held the theory that if a person has been abused, the only reference for self care they have is based on the pattern of abuse they have been brought up with. So it is possible for them, if the therapist is not aware of it, to do therapy in an abusive way and re-traumatise themselves. In Tasha's case, I feared she could have re-traumatised herself by watching the film Sybil.

✍ Tasha's timidity, with her almost zero self-esteem, was a key element that affected her greatly in many areas of her life. I wanted to focus on working on a way to help Tasha through this. I realised that when she impersonated her mother or spoke about her lack of trust in me or anyone, she was far from timid. In fact she was very confident. So the challenge was how to employ that confidence without the aggression.

✍ Every time Tash experienced anger as an emotion, her revulsion at it reduced her to a disabling level of timidity. As a defence strategy, in addition to this, Tasha's memory of her mother's anger paralysed her even further. So I felt that two main elements prevented her from moving beyond this point. Firstly there was her timidity, played out in valiant but misguided efforts to prevent her from becoming like her mother, despite the huge cost to her self-esteem. Secondly there was the real terrorising memory of her mother's frightening attacks on her.

✍ Tasha, because of her history of being abused, is full of rage and hate against her mother which for a long time could not be stated enough in our sessions. She wanted to hurt, humiliate. But this was predominantly unconscious in her and terrifying to face. To get near any kind of expression she would think of a pumpkin or a melon that she crushes, whacks or stabs, to give herself some sensory, therapeutic feedback.

 A major turning point in my work with Tasha came when she cried in the session where we had viewed the scene in Hope Floats together and were discussing her reaction. For me this was proof that a moment in a film can sometimes bring about in a person a powerful emotional reaction that therapy might take years to reach. It can provide the catalyst for the person to break through crippling and counter-productive defence mechanisms erected in early life.

MILLIE

Millie was a young mother who was agoraphobic. Her agoraphobia had been partially triggered by a film, A Nightmare on Elm Street, so her experience of film had been negative. In therapy, however, it proved possible to harness the power of film in a positive way using Bridget Jones' Diary and Four Weddings and a Funeral, and Millie's agoraphobia was cured.

Millie was a 'first' for me and her story of agoraphobia came as a slight shock. I was confronted with the negative power of film, which was also a first. Working with Millie I had a deadline as she was due to move house and therefore would have to go outside. She had a powerful imagination which fuelled her fear even more.

The phone rang one day.

"Hello, my name is Millie. I would like to have some sessions with you."

"OK, when can you come to see me?"

"Well, you see, that's the problem. I can't come to see you as I am agoraphobic."

This came as something of a shock to me, especially when I subsequently learned there was a 10 week deadline involved. Millie seemed so desperate that I decided to depart from my usual practice and do the sessions in her home.

When I arrived Millie was holding a young baby. I sat down among the toys and it was a very difficult way of working. I asked Millie why she could not go out. Was there something specific that had caused this? To my surprise she answered almost in a whisper, "If I go out, I'll go blind."

I asked her how long this had been going on. She told me she had not been out at all for two years and felt it had all started with an LSD trip that had gone very wrong. I asked her what had happened on the trip. She explained that she had got into a car and as she proceeded she felt these huge black lumps come out at her.

"Why do you connect that with your present phobia?" I asked.

"Well it just comes up and therefore I thought it might be of significance."

I was sure it was but gradually it became clear that there was something more. When I asked if she could think of any other incident that might be connected, Millie got very upset and started crying. It emerged that her brother-in-law had raped her after this LSD trip. She had kept this to herself, afraid to tell anyone.

When I asked why, it emerged that she was scared of breaking up her sister's marriage. Gradually in the session I began to see her as a person who copes and endures quietly, yet for some intuitive reason I did not feel that this was the issue. And to my surprise, in subsequent sessions, she was to tell me about an experience she'd had six years prior to the LSD trip and to being raped. She had been traumatised by the movie *A Nightmare on Elm Street* in which disfigured serial killer Freddy Krueger stalks a group of friends by appearing in their dreams.

A Nightmare on Elm Street seemed to be the origin of her phobia. This experience had made Millie stop taking baths as Freddy had held a woman under the water. Even now she would only have a shower. Freddy had made her terrified to go to sleep as that was the moment he would strike.

As I looked at Millie I was searching for a theme which seemed to be her desperate need to feel safe. If you fell asleep, you were no-longer in control. If you were in the bath you were extremely vulnerable. But Millie's agoraphobia meant she could control her environment and therefore have some semblance of safety. I also realised that as I was visiting her on her home ground, this was a more secure setting for her.

In subsequent sessions, relying on my antidote theory, I asked Millie what films had made her feel really good, comfortable and safe when she saw them. It was very interesting to observe Millie as she thought about all these films. A soft, warm glow came across her face as she talked about *Four Weddings and a Funeral* the romantic comedy that follows the fortunes of a group of friends, and *Bridget Jones' Diary* in which the unconfident Bridget is surrounded by a surrogate family of friends.

Once again I was looking for a common theme in these movies she had liked. The theme, it seemed, was sharing. As Millie talked about this, she started to sob again at the realisation of her loss of sharing with her very good friends. She had left them as a teenager to go off with − as she put it − 'a bad crowd'. She felt her friends would never like her again. It made her realise at that moment how important and powerful the emotional experience of sharing was.

I immediately started to think how I could now utilise this discovery about sharing as soon as possible in Millie's life, to help her to recover. I asked her to watch the films again and again because I wanted to get her in touch with what moved her about them.

I was most interested in her response to *Bridget Jones' Diary* because this was particularly strong. It appeared to offer a healing bridge from her present life to the sharing with friends that she had so identified with in the film. I hoped this experience would lead to her re-contacting her real friends.

I asked her about these friends. "Would it be possible for you to get in touch with them?" She thought for a moment. "They don't like me."

I asked her how long ago it had been since she had made contact with them and she said 10 years. "Don't you think you are in a time warp about this? A lot has gone on in their lives in 10 years and you are talking like you are a teenager again." She laughed at this realisation and said that she would think about contacting them.

I also asked her how she felt about the rape, and what came up in her when she thought about it. She started to cry. Then, in the middle of her tears, she said in a little girl's voice, "I want my mum." When I asked if she could ring her, she thought for a moment and said she could. I was asking if she could share this terrible secret with her mother when again she cried and repeated that she wanted her mum.

At this point in the therapy, I obviously realised that my suggestions were still maintaining the negative pattern of people coming to Millie as she wasn't going outside. But I was introducing the idea of new people, old friends, her mum, coming into her life again and all the important sharing and support that had moved her so deeply in the films that she had mentioned.

In the first couple of sessions I would meet Millie on her doorstep (just opening the door was terrifying for her in itself). Then, after she gained the courage to meet me there, I would get her to take two or three steps out onto the pavement. When she panicked I asked her to use the breathing technique I had taught her. Only when the technique started to work would I hold her hand in support.

My aim was to reinforce her confidence in the breathing techniques I had taught her to deal with her panic, gradually building up in her the early stages of control and safety.

Little by little I would lead her by the hand to the postbox about five yards from her house until I was eventually able to get her to meet me at the postbox with her arriving there first – something which took huge courage on her part. (I was actually parked across the road, out of her direct sight. I would wait a bit to see how she coped and if she was able to practice the breathing methods. Then, I would get out of the car and go to her.)

One day at the postbox as Millie went into her panic I asked her what was wrong at that moment. Taking gulps of air she replied, "I'm frightened of going blind." At this stage I felt our relationship was strong enough for what I was about to say. "OK Millie," I said, gently and firmly, "try now to go blind."

Millie looked deeply shocked but her breathing had settled down.

I said "How is it? Are you blind?"

"No," she whispered," "I just feel very dizzy."

"But you're telling me you've not gone blind?"

I then took her by the hand and led her back inside the house.

Although her thoughts were frightening, she now had the evidence and experience that she did not go blind. This, combined with the work we had done on sharing and the practice of her breathing method, allowed Millie to walk out further and further to meet me when I was not in view.

As the fear of going blind was subsiding and we entered into further sessions, she developed a new phobia that she could not breathe. She felt like she was fading – that she was going to die.

"OK Millie, I want you now to stop breathing and die!"

Millie looked utterly aghast and amazed. Gradually a twinkle appeared in her eye as she started to laugh. "I can't do it!"

I responded humorously, "Now, come on Millie, you are not really trying. Really try, stop that breathing altogether!"

After a time she took large gulps of air. Once again I pointed out to her that there was a pattern to her frightening thoughts but that her fear of dying, as with the blindness, would not materialise.

Millie's reaction to her own story

I had acquired Millie's permission to write up her story for this book. Yet when I showed her what I had written she exclaimed in surprise, "This is not me." After reading it intently she said, "The facts are all right but…"

"But you don't recognise your own behaviour?"

"Well, yes I do, but I am not like that."

I asked if she thought I had got her wrong. "No, no. It's difficult to explain," she said, deeply puzzled.

"Maybe," I suggested, "it is not who you are and feel, but it is your behaviour you don't recognise?"

"Yes," she said slowly, but I felt she was unconvinced.

I was fascinated by this reaction, feeling that it would be

very helpful to her therapy. It was showing her something about herself and her behaviour that was disconcerting in some way. She was seeing her behaviour from a third person perspective.

For me at that moment, the air was full of her unspoken questions.

"Is this really me? Is this what I have come to?" Somehow it was a kind of healthy shock for Millie.

Wanting to test her further, I asked a question to which I already knew the answer. "Do you want me to change what I have written Millie?" "No!" she said straight away, "not at all." She said this almost protectively of her story now.

We were coming towards the end of the session but I sensed that Millie was struggling to communicate her experience and that she needed time.

"Well, it is time to end now but think about it and we will talk about it next time."

She agreed and said that it had been helpful.

Venturing outside

I rang Millie today, as was my practice, to arrange for her to meet me on her own in the street — but this time up the hill where I would be sitting in my car. Each time I met her I had changed the place. But on this occasion, keeping the unpredictability while keeping up her confidence, I asked her to turn right up the hill instead of left as she usually did.

Millie was able to do this and I felt that this was a great step forward in her therapy. Holding her baby in her arms also seemed to provide some comfort and security. She seemed much calmer and you could feel there was an energetic breakthrough, with a complete change in her presence and body language and less anxiety than before.

It was interesting that she automatically brought the baby this time in the sense that she had given up using the excuse that she could not come out as she was on her own with the baby. Now she was bringing the baby with her without a word. I noticed in her manner a real sense of achievement that she had been able to take her baby out as other mothers do.

In previous conversations I had made the point that her baby daughter would subsequently take much more notice of what Millie said and did if she was taken out of the house by her as well as by her father. I think this had worried and motivated Millie to deal with her phobia as soon as possible.

The little girl was smiling and teasing her mum and they both looked very contented. Although we were only out for 10 minutes – a long time for Millie after not having come out at all for about two years – there were moments when mother and baby seemed perfectly happy. It was a joy to see and also, I think, an indicator of success.

This was about our ninth session and the interesting thing was that she now felt much better when she was out. A calm panic rather than a frantic panic came upon her, but she could control and manage it. Another interesting factor was that she now felt very uncomfortable indoors. It was a reversal of her original phobia, in that she said she could not breathe when inside the house.

Millie and her husband were getting ready to move from their very small, cramped flat and the passage was almost completely blocked with the fridge, washing machine and luggage. The state of the house did make you feel there was no room to breathe. Millie caught that feeling and understood that this may have been the reason for the way she was reacting.

Negative perceptions

I noticed Millie appeared able to take a normal event and twist the outcome. Her perceptions of situations were very negative and worrying to her. For example, if she felt a bit overwhelmed by all the furniture in her flat, or in a sense couldn't breathe, she would interpret this to mean that there was something wrong with her – that she was dying. The thought that she was dying would then make her more anxious and her breathing would become faster and more shallow, proving to her again that she felt worse inside the house. Her anxiety would go up and she would begin almost to hyperventilate.

I mentioned these things as we were walking back to her house and I asked her if there was any pattern in all of this. She said that she was starting to realise that it was to do with her mum.

She was becoming aware that unconciously she had latched onto her mother's pattern of thinking. Noticing this allowed her see herself from a different perspective. I put it to her that what had been learned could be unlearned. In the same way films that had a frightening effect on her because of her powerful imagination could be countered by 'antidote' films that had a positive impact.

I explained that she could use any film that made her feel better as a constant resource, until she naturally integrated the sense of wellbeing created in her by the film just by thinking about it rather than needing actually to see it.

In one session where I asked Millie to watch *Bridget Jones' Diary* it became increasingly clear that it was the sharing of friendship that was so important to her in both *Bridget Jones* and in *Four Weddings and a Funeral*.

I encouraged her to go on the internet to re-establish contact with her friends she had lost. My long-term aim was to get her to go out and meet these friends again. In the meantime I though she could reconnect and still feel safe.

Her old friends responded very positively when contacted. By initiating this renewed contact and by enrolling in a home media course (inspired, she said, by *Bridget Jones*) Millie was breaking out of the bubble she had found herself in and was gradually getting her life back. I encouraged her to watch *Bridget Jones' Diary* over and over so that it repeatedly infused in her a sense of hope and sharing and could serve as a resource for her even when I wasn't around.

I asked Millie about when she had read her case study and had said, "This is not me." She said she had recognised herself, but that it was not who she really was. I told Millie I thought this represented an important experience as it was helping her to see herself differently – to discern the difference between her true self and her behaviour. She said she found this insight very helpful and would think about it in more detail.

Bridget Jones' Diary

Following our sessions Millie explained in her own words how the film Bridget Jones' Diary had helped her.

"I feel almost jealous of Bridget. I envy her lifestyle and personality. I envy the way she was brought up, her job and her friends. I would like to be her.

"I feel almost involved with her group of friends. As if I am part of the group, although sometimes I feel like the looker-on, yearning to get in, almost like the geek at school wanting to get into the 'in crowd'.

"Daniel, the rogue boyfriend, is the kind of man I would be interested in.

"I find the film almost inspires me to get the career I would enjoy and hopefully one with the social scene I want. It makes me sad, as I hate the social scene I have access to at the moment.

"I really feel as if I could fit in with these people and their social scene.

"I feel like I want the beginning of a relationship again.

"When Bridget finds Daniel is cheating on her it brings back a lot of memories of how she felt and I was envious that she had great friends to help her get through it while I had nobody at all.

"My favourite scenes are those where Bridget and her boss are emailing each other and where Bridget and Daniel go on a weekend break and are mucking about on the boating lake."

Case Notes

✍ This case study ends rather abruptly in the same way that Millie decided
   to end with me. I had worked effectively with her and her phobia for 10
   weeks in a behavioural style, but that did not mean that the transference
   wasn't activated on me as a good dad. As her real dad had abandoned
   her, when I went on holiday all her unconscious anger came out that
   once again she had been abandoned by a man. And although Millie
   gave me her new address and phone number before I went on holiday, I
   was never able to make contact or get her to answer my calls again.

✍ Millie and I did good work together and I hope she continues to be free
   of her phobia which is what brought her to me. But ongoing broader
   psychotherapy would have helped her with emotional issues which had
   not been dealt with and of which her phobia was merely a symptom.

✍ Millie's willingness to work in a behavioural way with me was prompted
   by her anxiety that, although she was too frightened to go outside, she
   was due to move house in 10 weeks' time. These are the kind of
   complexities therapists face. This example once again shows the
   unconscious attack on the therapist, in this case as the abandoning
   father. Consciously Millie would probably have had very good practical
   reasons for limiting her therapy like cost and the fact that she was feeling
   much better. She would have been unaware of her unconscious
   motivations.

CONCLUSION

The Value of Movie Therapy

Movie therapy can be a therapeutic resource (see Tasha) and a powerful catalyst for identifying and expressing troublesome emotions (see Mac). It can help us to see where our unhealthy attitudes and patterns of behaviour will lead us if we don't change but through a therapeutic experience that can actually help us change (see Bette, Susi).

Movie therapy is a helpful way of communicating difficult emotions to others in our relationships. For example Bette was able to explain gently to her husband about how her mother-in-law made her feel by showing him a clip from the film *Rebecca* featuring Mrs. Danvers.

Movie therapy helps us to identify complex emotions and frees us from them. It does this by giving them expression in a way that reduces their emotional charge and produces more clarity. It helps us to better manage our emotions.

Spiritually it can help us witness our egoic processes from another level of consciousness as in Buddhist mindfulness. It can help us develop a place of self awareness from which we can witness our thoughts and feelings without being sucked in and contaminated by them.

A TESTIMONY

In these extracts from an email Bette,
whose case study features in this
book, explains what effect movies
have had on her emotional life and
thinking, and how they have enriched
her experience of therapy.

When I met Bernie Wooder I was depressed, confused and lacked self-confidence. I found this difficult to understand. I had all the things I thought would make me happy but I didn't feel happy. Bernie encouraged me to explore how I felt rather than what I was thinking and to express these feelings. I was surprised to find parts of me that I didn't know I had because I had denied these aspects of me. This allowed me to get a better sense of who I was and what was important to me. I now feel as if I know myself better than I ever have before. I am no longer depressed or confused and my self-confidence has increased.

Bernie's calm understanding and intelligent approach made it easy for me to feel comfortable experiencing all my feelings, anger, pain, hurt, fear etc.

I am now happy with myself and my life, even though not everything in my life is perfect. I have learnt new ways to cope with life. My weekly sessions with Bernie keep me in touch with who I am and what I want.

Bernie's approach to my therapy took many different forms. When I was experiencing difficulties with my husband's ex-wife, he suggested I watch Alfred Hitchcock's film Rebecca. I did this and read Daphne Du Maurier's book. I found this very helpful. It allowed me to see some of the feelings I was experiencing and I talked about them with Bernie. We used books and films frequently. I found The Wedding Singer contained scenes which portrayed how I felt and by watching this and talking about it I felt very reassured.

Bernie provided me with an environment where I could express all of my feelings and from this experience I was able to let go of these negative feelings and move on. I was allowed to be who I am. Although this did help me through a difficult patch, it didn't help me to make the necessary long-term changes that were required. Bernie gave me the parenting I didn't have.

I was scared about telephoning Bernie to arrange an appointment and petrified about attending this meeting. And this didn't really change upon meeting him for the first time. At first I found Bernie quite scary. But now, looking back, I think this was more about me than about him. I have always found Bernie to be approachable, patient and sympathetic.

Our first session consisted of Bernie asking me questions about myself and my past. I found it easy to answer the questions but they didn't help me to feel better. I felt incredibly desperate to feel better and had hoped I would start to feel different immediately. But I didn't, and this impatience proved to be one of the many issues that Bernie and I worked on to help me.

I had expected Bernie to be soft, friendly and 'bean baggy'. However, he was direct and straightforward. I found this approach helpful because I had respect for Bernie right from the start and didn't see him as a 'liberal social worker type'. I didn't feel entirely comfortable with him at the beginning. But, looking back now I'm not sure it would have been possible to feel completely at ease immediately with anyone. The feelings I needed to express were very painful and I needed to trust the person I was going to seek help from with this process. I found in time that I did trust Bernie. He always listened to how I felt, never made any judgement of me and didn't always 'take my side'. This helped my trust in him to grow.

Films continue to play and important and helpful part in my life. Whilst watching Titanic for the second time a couple of months ago I made the following notes:

It has occurred to me that Rose's story (Rose is played by Kate Winslet) has some similarities with my own life. Although Titanic is essentially a love story, it strikes a different chord with me. I identify with the situation Rose is in. She is feeling trapped and unhappy.

The scene that particularly sticks out for me is the one in which Rose goes to the party below deck after Jack has joined Rose, her family and friends for dinner. Jack's words to Rose whilst they are dancing below deck were 'Don't think, just feel'. I couldn't help but smile for Rose and I realised I was smiling for myself too. She really let go and enjoyed herself at the party. Allowing herself to be truly who she is. Something I need to remember to do for myself more frequently.

Rose felt trapped by her life, soon to marry Cal, a rich man who, she was beginning to realise, she didn't love. Rose's mother, noticing she was starting to break free, reminded her that she needed to marry Cal because her father had died leaving debts. Rose's mother accused her of being selfish. This mirrors the emotional blackmail my mother at times used with me. And it was Rose's mother who was, in fact, being selfish by thinking of herself.

Rose, a passionate, warm, life loving person, couldn't fit into the space her mother and fiancée allowed her to live in. This is similar to my family situation. I wish my name were Rose too.

Another scene that sticks out is the one in which Rose's mother gets on the lifeboat and the way that Rose says goodbye to her mother. It appears to be said with both anger and relief. She then runs off to find Jack who had been arrested for stealing the 'heart of the ocean' necklace.

Movies chosen by clients whose stories are told in the book

The Beach (2000) with Leonardo DiCaprio, Tilda Swinton.
Twenty-something Richard travels to Thailand and finds himself in possession of a strange map, supposedly leading to a solitary beach paradise. Excited and intrigued, he sets out to find it.

The Bridges of Madison County (1995) with Meryl Streep, Clint Eastwood.
The children of Francesca Johnson are going through her possessions after her death. They discover her diary, love letters and various keepsakes revealing her intense, four-day love affair with a photographer Robert Kincaid who had drifted into town on an assignment.

Bridget Jones' Diary (2001) with Renée Zellweger, Hugh Grant, Colin Firth.
A single woman in her 30s living in London, Bridget Jones is struggling against her age, her weight, her job, and (as she sees it) her many imperfections. She is surrounded by a surrogate family of friends but lacks confidence in herself and with men until a romantic entanglement with her smarmy boss Daniel Cleaver, and later with stiff upper lip barrister, Mark Darcy, give her a whole new perspective.

Four Weddings and a Funeral (1994) with Hugh Grant, Andie MacDowell.
Charles is a confirmed British bachelor – one of a close-knit group of friends who share the big moments in their lives. He meets the perfect woman, Carrie, at a friend's wedding and

although the two continue to cross paths, they never find each other at a time when both are available.

The Go-Between (1970) with Julie Christie, Alan Bates.
In the summer of 1900 young Leo, guest of a wealthy classmate at a grand country home in Norfolk, is befriended by his friend's beautiful sister Marian. Though engaged to a Viscount, Marian is conducting an affair with their rakish neighbour Ted Burgess, and Leo, asked to carry messages between them, rapidly loses his innocence as he realises he is being used.

Hope Floats (1998) with Sandra Bullock.
After her husband reveals his infidelity to her in a TV talk show and walks out on her, a young woman takes her daughter and goes home to her mother in the small town in Smithville, Texas where she grew up.

Life is Beautiful (1997) with Roberto Benigni, Giorgio Cantarini.
A Jewish Italian father, Guido Orefice, learns how to use his fertile imagination to help his son survive their internment in a Nazi con-centration camp.

The Lord of the Rings (2001-2003) Trilogy with Elijah Wood, Viggo Mortensen, Ian McKellen.
In a small village in the Shire in the fictional world of Middle-earth, a young Hobbit named Frodo has been entrusted with an ancient Ring. He and a fellowship of friends and allies embark on an epic quest to the Cracks of Doom in order to

destroy it and thus ensure the end of its maker, the dark Lord Sauron.

Monty Python's Life of Brian (1979) with Graham Chapman and the Monty Python comedy team.
Brian is born on the original Christmas, in the stable next door. He is mistaken for the messiah and spends his life being manipulated, abused, and exploited by various religious and political factions in this sharp satire on religious zealotry and hypocrisy.

A Nightmare on Elm Street (1984) with John Saxon, Heather Langenkamp.
On Elm Street, Nancy Thompson and a group of her friends are being tormented in their dreams by a clawed killer named Freddy Krueger who tries to pick off his victims one by one.

On Golden Pond (1981) with Katharine Hepburn, Henry Fonda, Jane Fonda.
An ageing couple Ethel and Norman Thayer, who spend each summer at their cottage on Golden Pond, are visited by daughter Chelsea with her fiancé and his rebelious son. The son stays on, bonds with Norman, and Chelsea sees their developing relationship as the one she missed with her father when she was growing up.

Priscilla, Queen of the Desert (1994) with Terence Stamp, Hugo Weaving, Guy Pearce.
Three drag queens (two gay men and a transsexual woman)

drive across the Australian outback from Sydney to Alice Springs in a large bus they have named Priscilla.

Rebecca (1940) with Laurence Olivier, Joan Fontaine.
When a young woman marries a rich widower and settles in his gigantic mansion, she finds him and the servants still in the grip of the memory of his first wife, Rebecca. The second Mrs De Winter feels eclipsed by the sophisticated Rebecca, and is hated by the housekeeper Mrs Danvers who loved Rebecca and was in awe of her.

The Remains of the Day (1993) with Anthony Hopkins, Emma Thompson.
Emotionally repressed butler Mr Stevens is too frightened to express his love for housekeeper Miss Kenton and by the time he gathers enough courage to tell her of his feelings she has left her employment at Darlington Hall where they both work. Years later he goes in search of her.

Shadowlands (1993) with Anthony Hopkins, Debra Winger.
C S Lewis, world-renowned writer and academic, leads a passionless life as an Oxford don until in his mid-50s he meets spirited American poet Joy Gresham. She is an extrovert while he is oh-so-English and inhibited but her coaxing and personality gradually draw him out to express himself more, both more emotionally and physically.

Shirley Valentine (1989) with Pauline Collins, Tom Conti.
Shirley's a middle-aged Liverpool housewife who finds herself

talking to the wall while she prepares dinner for her husband, wondering what happened to her life. But when her best friend wins an all-expenses-paid vacation, she plucks up the courage to pack her bags, leave drudgery behind and heads for Greece where she begins to see the world, and herself, in a different light.

The Sound of Music (1965) with Julie Andrews, Christopher Plummer.

In 1930s Austria, on the eve of WWII, a young woman leaves a convent to become governess to the seven children of a navy captain who is a widower. Initially met with some hostility by the children, her kindness, understanding, and sense of fun soon draws them to her and brings some much-needed joy into all their lives – including the captain's.

Star Wars (1977) with Mark Hamill, Harrison Ford, Alec Guiness.

In a faraway galaxy, a psychopathic emperor and his most trusted servant – a former Jedi Knight known as Darth Vader – are ruling a universe with fear. They have built a horrifying weapon known as the Death Star, a giant battle station capable of annihilating a world in less than a second; but the Death Star's master plans are captured by the fledgling Rebel Alliance.

Sybil (1976) with Sally Field, Joanne Woodward.

A shy young graduate student, Sybil Dorsett, suffers from dissociative identity disorder because of an abusive early life.

With the help of her psychiatrist, Sybil gradually recalls the harrowing childhood abuse that led to the development of 16 different personalities, including some which made her appear psychotic, and one that even made her want to kill herself.

Titanic (1997) with Leonardo DiCaprio, Kate Winslett.
Jack Dawson and Rose DeWitt Bukater are two members of different social classes who fall in love aboard the ill-fated RMS Titanic on the luxury cruise ship's 1912 maiden voyage.

The Truman Show (1998) with Jim Carrey, Ed Harris.
Truman Burbank grows up in the small town of Seahaven, unaware that it is actually the set of a successful television reality show and that his life has been broadcast around the world since the day he was born. He becomes suspicious that all is not what it seems and makes a bid for freedom.

Watership Down (1978). Animated feature film.
A group of rabbits flee their doomed warren and face many dangers in their search for a new home. While they eventually find a peaceful spot at Watership Down, they soon find themselves in a deadly conflict with the neighbouring warren called Efrafa, a police state run by the powerful and insane General Woundwart.

The Wedding Singer (1998) with Adam Sandler.
Robbie, the singer, and Julia, the waitress, are both engaged to be married – but to the wrong people. Fortune intervenes to help them discover each other.